A TOTAL PERCUSSION APPROACH TO PLAYING THE DRUMSET

GLENN KOTCHE

Alfred Music
P.O. Box 10003
Van Nuys, CA 91410-0003
alfred.com

ISBN-10: 0-7390-9955-8
ISBN-13: 978-0-7390-9955-1

TABLE OF CONTENTS

INTRODUCTION

The underlying concept of *A Beat a Week* is a total-percussion approach to drumset. After college, when I began to play professionally, I found that I had the most success when I started to incorporate ideas, techniques, and even instruments from all the various styles of music that I'd previously played and studied. I applied skills from concert, world, and marching percussion as well as jazz, rock, funk, and electronic idioms. This comprehensive approach allowed me to find my creative voice and effectively utilize it musically.

A Beat a Week contains 52 unique beats—spanning 15 years of my recorded catalog—that exemplify this approach. This book was written with the intent of being a supplemental drumset method that fosters creativity in players of all ages without requiring an extensive time commitment. The beats range from basic to advanced; each has a unique twist that illustrates the balance between functionality and musical inventiveness. Beats are grouped according to unifying characteristics, which allows you to work through the book as written or by skipping around its various chapters.

The detailed text that accompanies each beat explains its inspiration, origins, and evolution. By illuminating the thought process behind these beats, students gain a deeper understanding of approaches that can be applied to their own creative musical situations.

Most of the examples are broken down step-by-step, identifying and exposing any potential physical hurdles. This "divide-and-conquer" process has proven crucial for me to continue to teach myself new ideas and advanced concepts and I hope it will assist readers of this book in the same way. Additional examples of related material from across the percussion spectrum encourage an understanding of how seemingly disparate or unrelated ideas can be applied to drumset performance. This book is intended for drummers of all experience levels or anyone simply curious about the creative process.

Drumset Legend

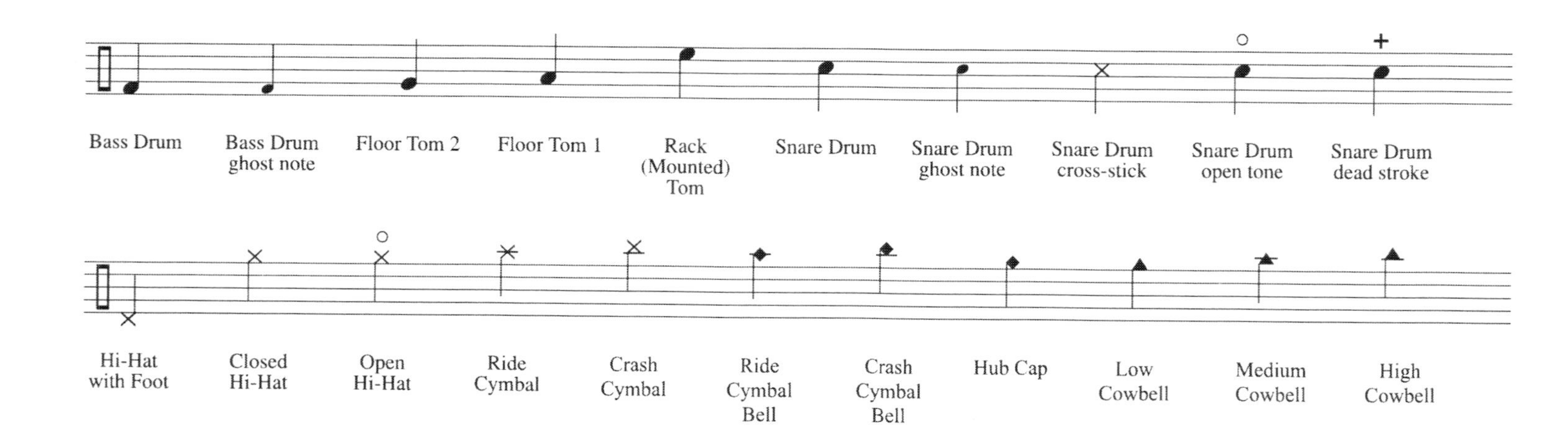

CHAPTER 1

Ride Interpretations
Part 1

ONE WING (bridge)

Wilco from *Wilco (The Album)*

Our first beat is from the bridge section of the song "One Wing." This is a fairly straight-ahead beat with one small exception: the hi-hat part (I play it with my right hand) has an accent pattern that gives the beat a sort of melody. I refer to this as a melodic ride.

Example 1A: One Wing (Bridge 2:06)

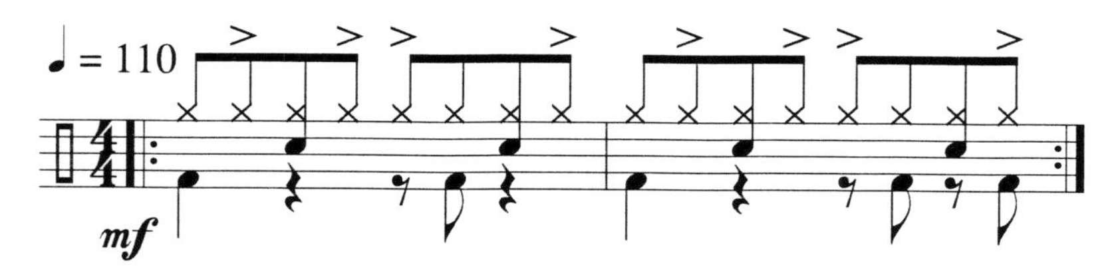

Here is an example of the beat without the hi-hat melody.

Example 1B: Straight Hi-Hat Part

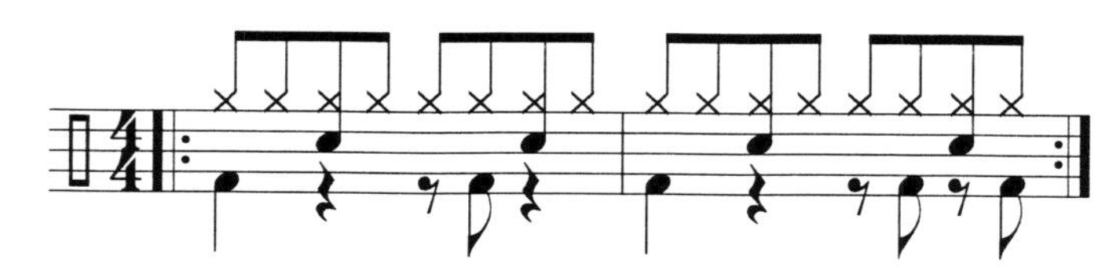

Next, a breakdown is shown between the melodic hi-hat part and the snare, just to make sure the accents are isolated and distinct from the unaccented notes. I emphasize these accents quite a bit, creating a big difference in height and volume between the accented and unaccented hi-hat notes.

Example 1C: Melodic Hi-Hat and Snare Drum

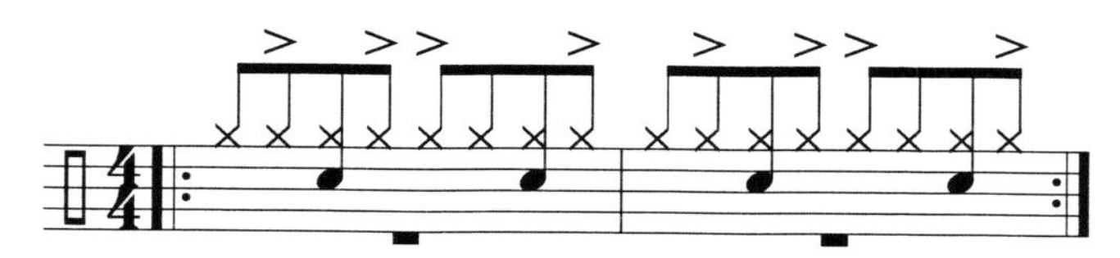

And finally, a breakdown is shown between the hi-hat part and the bass drum. This exposes the only potentially tricky part of the beat—the last eighth-note subdivision in the second measure. All of the other hi-hat accents are independent of the bass drum, but here the bass drum and hi-hat accents happen together. This doesn't seem too tough, but since a bass drum note without an accented hi-hat immediately follows, there's a tendency to add a hi-hat accent on beat 1 where it shouldn't be. Be careful of that and, again, make sure there's a noticeable difference in the volume and stroke-height of the accented and unaccented hi-hat notes, otherwise the hi-hat melody won't come through.

Example 1D: Melodic Hi-Hat and Bass Drum

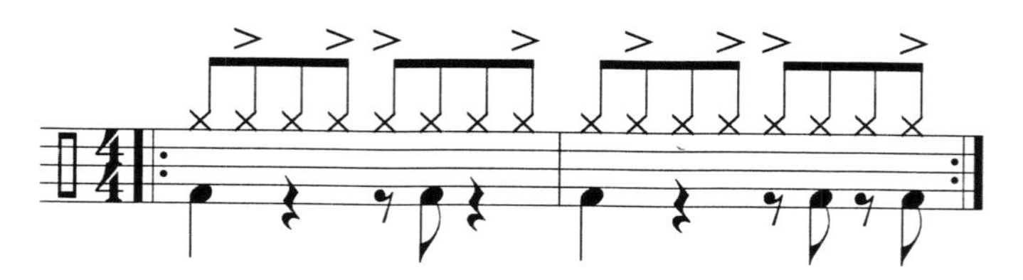

This is a beat I use all the time. Slight variations of it also appear in the live versions of the Wilco songs "Kamera" and "A Shot in the Arm." In fact, it was when we were mixing "Kamera" that I came up with this beat. Mixing engineer Jim O'Rourke put some compression on the drum track and all of a sudden these accents appeared where the drums weren't playing. I loved the way it sounded, so I began to emulate that when we played it live, adding an extra accent as well just because it felt a little better that way.

If you're up for it, you can always try the hi-hat part in examples 1A, 1C, and 1D by playing only the accents and leaving out all of the unaccented or "inner beats," as they are sometimes called. And, I strongly recommend you pick a simple bass drum/snare beat of your own and experiment with different accent patterns in the ride part.

WEEK 2

YOU NEVER KNOW

Wilco from *Wilco (The Album)*

This song has a nice stomp to it, similar to the song "Everyday People" by Sly & the Family Stone, along with elements of George Harrison's "My Sweet Lord." For the chorus beat of the song, I take a basic beat and change up the ride or right-hand part. Instead of keeping time with constant pulsing eighth notes, there's a bit more space in the ride part that emphasizes counts 1 and 3. I then split it up so the ride part alternates between the cymbal bell and the floor tom. This creates a nice counterpoint against the 2 and 4 snare drum back beat and infuses a little melodic element into the beat for the choruses.

Example 2A: You Never Know (Chorus 0:53)

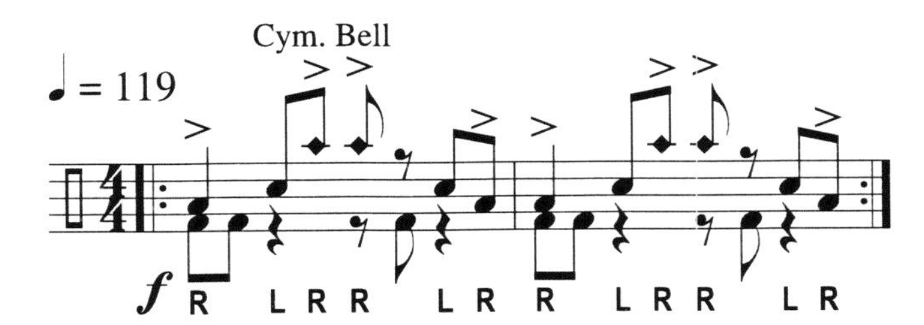

To better illustrate this, let's go through some breakdowns (leaving certain voices out of the beat) so we can see how everything fits together. First, try just the snare and bass drum parts.

Example 2B: Snare Drum and Bass Drum Only

The next example shows how the right hand alternates between high (cymbal bell) and low (floor tom).

Example 2C: Cymbal Bell and Floor Tom* (Right Hand Only)

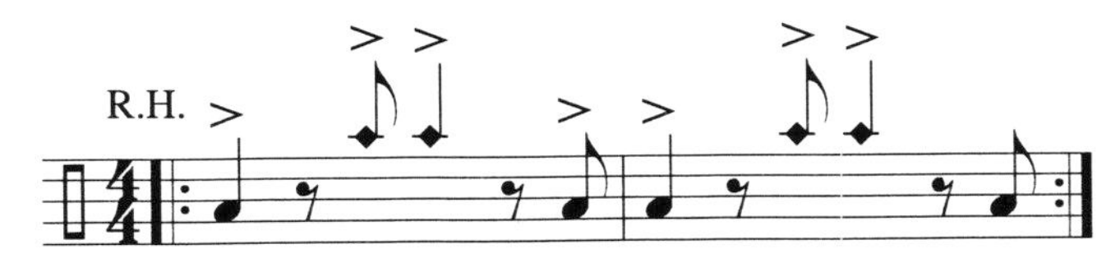

The final two examples show the melodic right-hand part isolated against both the snare drum and the bass drum part.

Example 2D: Bell and Floor Tom with Snare Drum

Example2E: Bell and Floor Tom with Bass Drum

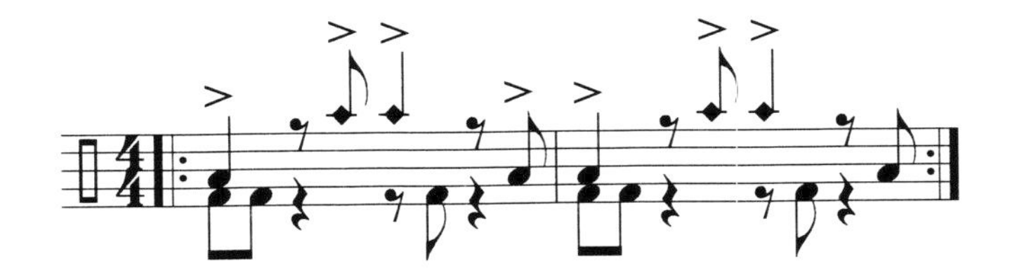

SPIDERS (KIDSMOKE)

Wilco from *A Ghost Is Born*

This is a driving motoric song inspired by what is lovingly referred to as Krautrock, a genre that groups together some of my favorite bands like Can, Kraftwerk, Faust, and Amon Düül.

To emphasize the relentless forward motion of this music, the beat for "Spiders" features constant eighth notes on the bass drum, along with a simple quarter-note ride pattern played on the hi-hat and a standard snare back beat on counts 2 and 4. The little twist I do to keep it from being too anchored on the downbeats is to add accents on all of the bass drum upbeats. This seems simple enough. We play accents with our hands all the time, but not too frequently with our feet—or at least not enough in my opinion!

Example 3A: Spiders (Verse)

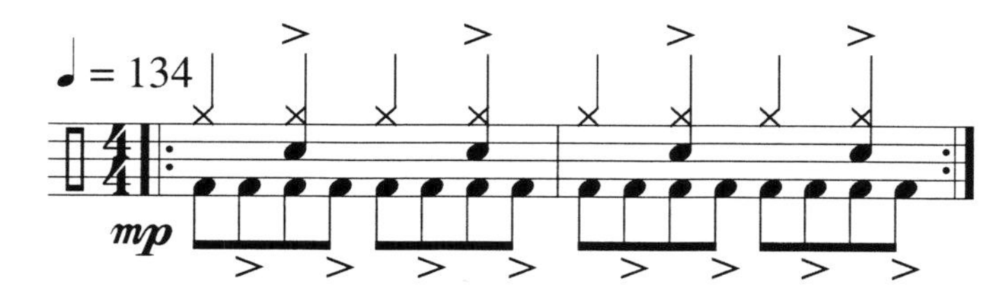

In order to pull this off at this tempo, I end up sort of bouncing the beater off of the head and emphasizing every other note (almost like a Moeller stroke with the foot). Experiment on your own, but I've noticed that when I do this, I tend to swivel my heel off of the pedal board to the right for accented notes (but keeping the ball of my foot stationary on the pedal board), and swivel it back to the left to place it on the pedal board for unaccented notes. But again, try achieving it in a variety of ways, and always just go with what feels natural and comfortable for you.

Example 3B: Without Snare Drum

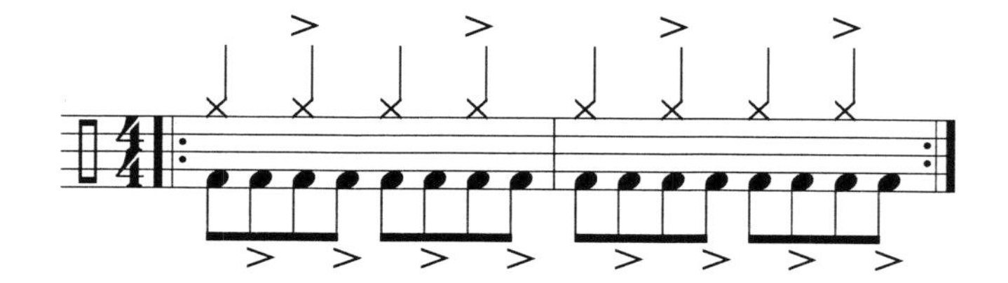

WEEK 4

I'LL FIGHT

Wilco from *Wilco (The Album)*

Similar to the last beat from "Spiders," the beat for "I'll Fight" also has a constant eighth-note pulse throughout, except this time it's on the snare drum. I've found that on certain types of songs and at the right tempo, reinforcing the traditional eighth note ride-cymbal pattern by doubling it on the snare drum can add a sense of solidity and strengthen the overall groove. It's subtle enough that it might be more felt than heard, but in my experience it works and unifies everything.

Example 4A: I'll Fight (Verse 0:18)

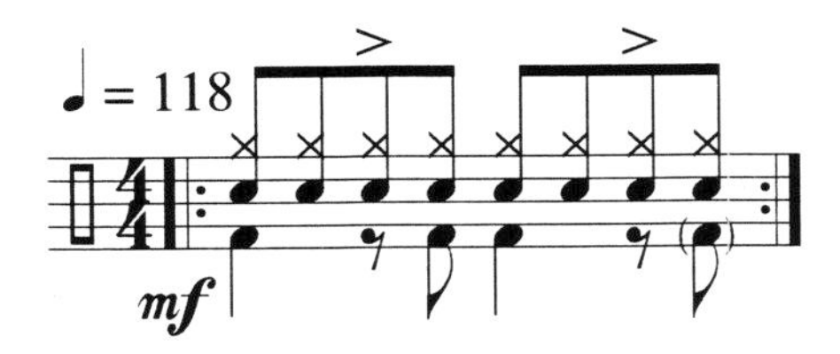

If you strip away the snare drum/ride double, you get a common beat.

Example 4B: Without Snare Drum Reinforcement

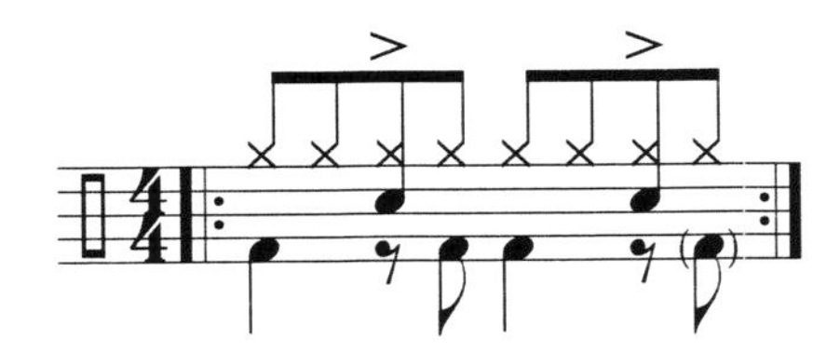

I tend to accent both the hi-hat and snare drum on counts 2 and 4, but it's good to able to accent the snare alone as well.

Example 4C: Hands Only

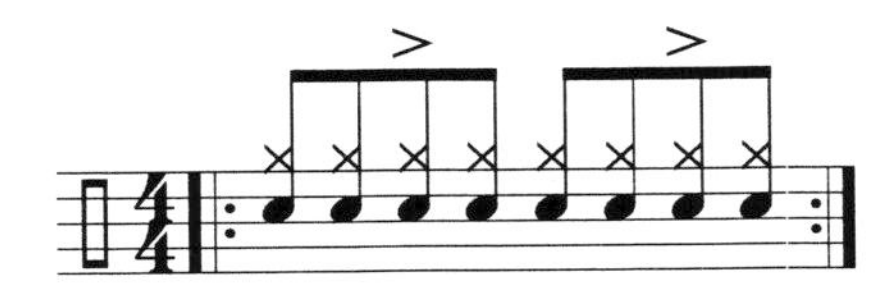

I was first exposed to the idea of a part being more felt than heard while learning big band drumming in college. It was common practice in the earlier days of big bands (the '20s and '30s) to keep a steady pulse on the bass drum and not just the ride cymbal. It has a unifying effect on the band and glues everything together by providing a subtle, low-end anchor. Here's an example of what I'm talking about. This is the same idea, but just in a different style of music and on a different voice of the drumset.

Example 4D: Implied Bass Drum

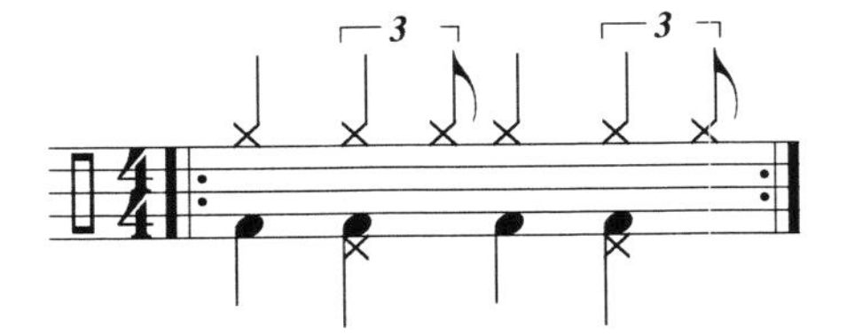

CHAPTER 2

Ride Interpretations
Part 2

FRUITA

birddog from *Ghost of the Season*

This song features a more sensitive drum part, so as not to overpower the acoustic guitar and cello. I use a brush in the left hand for the back beat on a snare (with the snares turned off), which gives it a warmer and more understated timbre. Instead of keeping time on the hi-hat or ride cymbal, I split the ride part between the floor tom and snare drum (which functions more like a tenor drum when the snares are turned off). I found it easier and more economical to hold two mallets in my right hand—one for the floor tom and the other for the snare drum—instead of constantly shifting my hand between the two surfaces. Notice that the feet and left hand are playing in regular time with accents on beats 2 and 4, while the right hand implies a half-time feel with an accent on beat 3. I like to juxtapose two time feels when it makes sense musically.

Example 5A: Fruita (Verse 0:18)
(Left Hand = Snares Off with Brush / Right Hand = Mallets)

And, here's an isolated example (with only the hands) showing which mallet is playing which drum. I'm calling the inside mallet #1 and the outside #2.

Example 5B: Hands Only

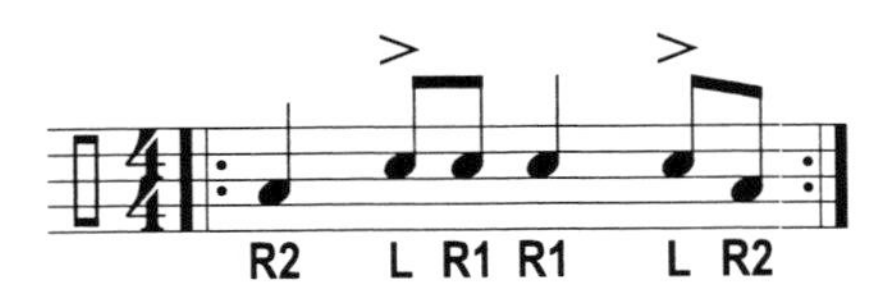

If you forego using the mallets, toms, and the brush, here's what the beat looks like if it were played more traditionally with the right hand on the hi-hat.

Example 5C: Full Beat, but with Right Hand Playing Hi-Hat

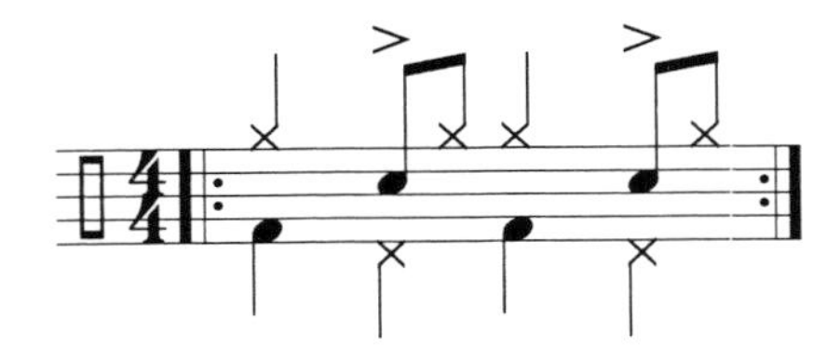

While playing this beat, you might find a similarity to an earlier example from the song "You Never Know." In that song the right hand alternates between the cymbal bell and the floor tom. Here the difference in pitch is between the floor tom and the higher pitched tenor drum. I find a correlation between this aspect of the beat and playing the surdo (Brazilian bass drum). The surdo is hung by a strap over the shoulder and is usually played with a single mallet. The free hand not holding the mallet dampens the head on alternating beats, creating an open/closed alternating. This is for the most basic surdo pattern. Using two distinct alternating sounds is a common feature of drumming in many cultures. Whether it's the alternating high and low sound of African bells, the surdo, conga slaps and open tones, pandiero open and closed tones, or the bass and snare drums in rock music, there's universality to this musical trait. Here is an example of that basic surdo pattern, as well as two other variations.

Example 5D: Surdo

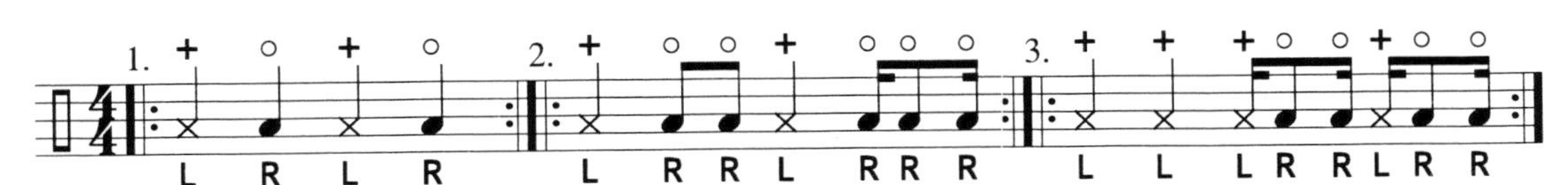

WEEK 6

I'M A WHEEL

Wilco from *A Ghost Is Born*

This is a straight ahead, up-tempo rock song. The bass drum part will be challenging to some because of the fast tempo and three consecutive fast eighth notes.

Example 6A: I'm a Wheel (Verse 0:07)

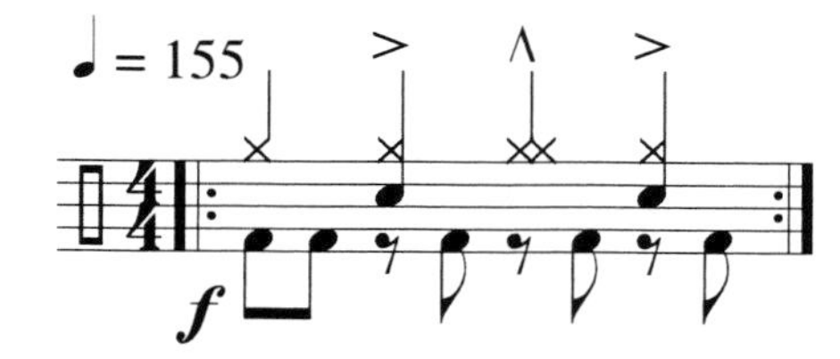

Besides the emphasis on 2 and 4 (the back beat), I also accent the hi-hats on beat 3. This is achieved by playing a double stop, in which both hands play together at the same volume (unlike a flam in which one hand plays a fraction before the other, and usually from a much lower height). Here is the left-hand part.

Example 6B: Left Hand Only

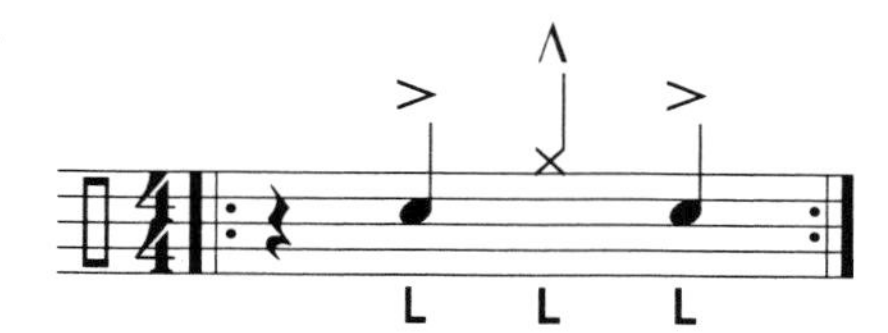

So, you can see that the left hand just moves over from the snare drum to the hi-hat, plays a slightly louder accent, and then moves back to the snare drum. Once this becomes comfortable, add the right hand.

Example 6C: Hands Only

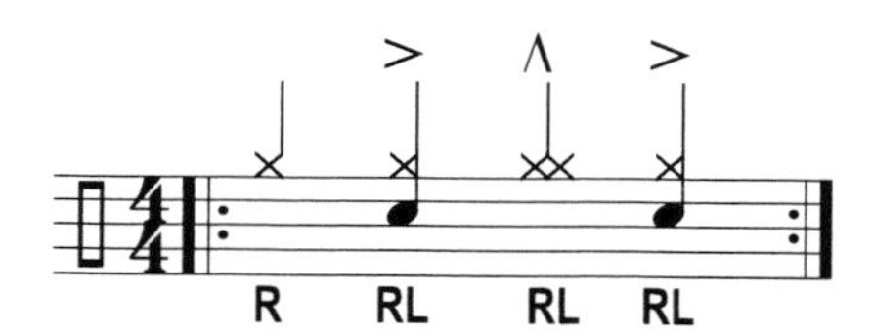

It's not a difficult beat, but that extra hi-hat double stop gives the beat a bit more personality, and makes it a lot of fun to play as well.

ART OF ALMOST (ending)

Wilco from *The Whole Love*

This is the beat from the coda/double-time ending section of this song. It's quite a bit different from the main beat and is basically an all-out ending freak-out beat. It's similar to the last beat from "I'm a Wheel" in that it's fast, and I also move my left hand back and forth between the snare drum and hi-hat.

Example 7A: Art of Almost (Ending 6:08)

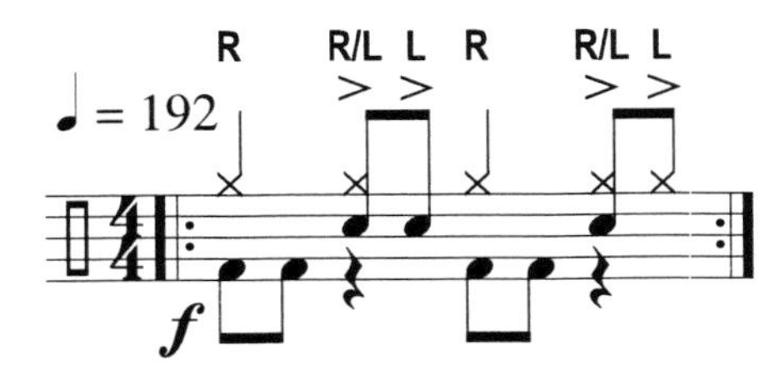

Counts 2 and 4 have the same left-hand rhythm but are voiced differently. I find that by doing this instead of playing the hi-hat accent on the "+" subdivision of beat 4 with my right hand, the accent is much more powerful and pronounced, which is key since the whole band is playing at maximum energy and volume at this point in the song.

Example 7B: Left Hand Only

Once the left-hand movement between the snare and hi-hat becomes comfortable, try adding the bass drum as well. Once you get this, all you need to add are quarter notes on the hi-hat with the right hand.

Example 7C: Left Hand and Bass Drum

BORN ALONE (verse)

Wilco from *The Whole Love*

For this beat, I shift the time-keeping away from the right hand or the ride part. Instead, I keep a steady eighth-note pulse on the bass drum throughout most of the song. This frees up the hands to try a few different things in various sections of the song. One of these is alternating between hi-hat openings of different lengths.

Example 8A: Born Alone (Verse 0:48)

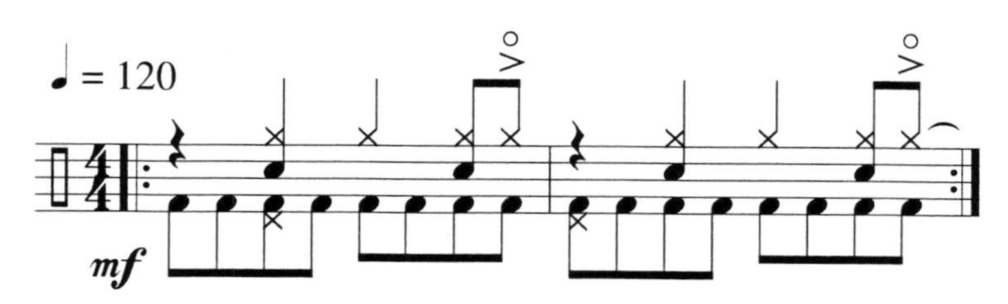

As you can see, this is a two-measure repeating beat with a hi-hat opening on the "+" subdivision of beat 4 in each measure. In the first measure, the opening is short (only an eighth note long). But in the second measure, by contrast, I let the hi-hats ring out and don't close them again until beat 2 of the following measure. That opening, therefore, lasts for the duration of three eighth notes. Check out the following example, which takes the bass drum out of the equation so you can concentrate on the hi-hat openings. Notice that the hi-hat, when played with the pedal, is also written to show when the opening stops.

Example 8B: Without Bass Drum

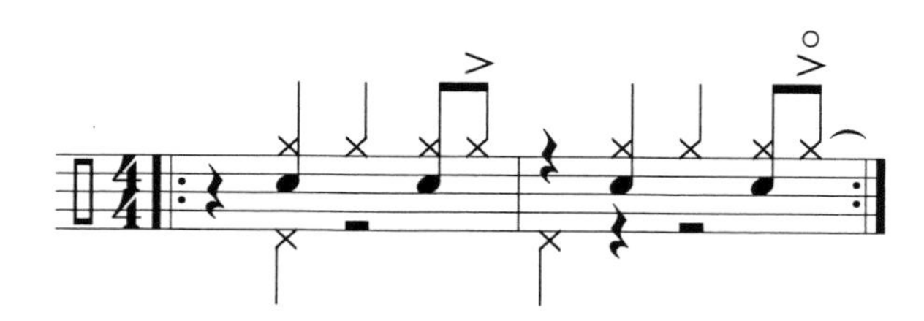

And finally, try it without the actual hi-hat openings so you can just concentrate on how the bass drum matches up with the hi-hat when played with the left foot.

Example 8C: Without Right Hand on Hi-Hat

CHAPTER 3

Beats with Implied Meters

EVERYTHING THAT GLITTERS

Paul K & The Weathermen from *Love Is a Gas*

This song has a swung, half-time $^{12}_{8}$ feel. The beat on the verse is fairly straightforward with the exception of a few snare drum drags thrown in on the upbeats after the back beat. I've found that adding these little upbeat drags helps to establish the tempo and feel. For the chorus, the whole song opens up a bit and the beat implies a 2 over 3 feel. For some reason it seems right to give up riding on the cymbal at this point and move the time to the snare drum—specifically an open snare drum roll with accents that play off of Paul K.'s preceding vocal phrasing.

It's a good idea to get the feel down first. So, let's try this with all of the elements (including the snare accents), but sans the snare roll. I've included examples in both $^{6}_{8}$ time and in $^{3}_{4}$ so you can choose which is most comfortable for you.

Example 9A: Everything that Glitters

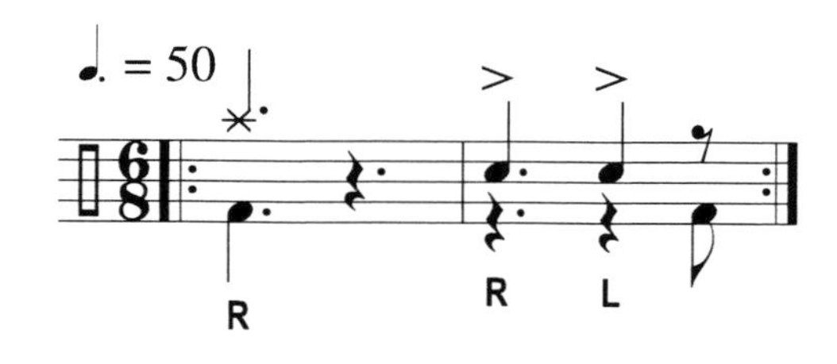

Example 9B: Written in $^{3}_{4}$

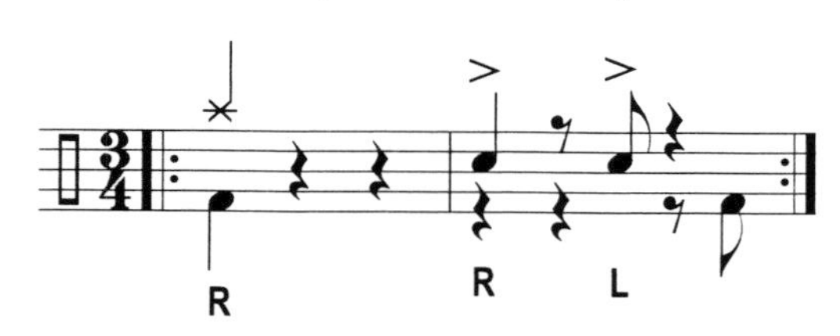

Next, let's try the hands, but all on one surface—the snare drum. I keep the rolls open with discernable subdivisions, as opposed to a buzz, press, or closed roll. At this tempo, you could actually play single strokes in place of the open rolls, especially if open rolls aren't your forte. Again, the examples are the same, but in two different meters.

Example 9C: Hands Only

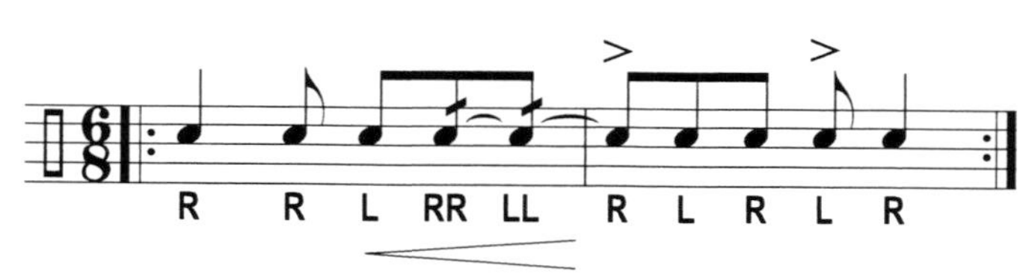

Example 9D: Written in $^{3}_{4}$

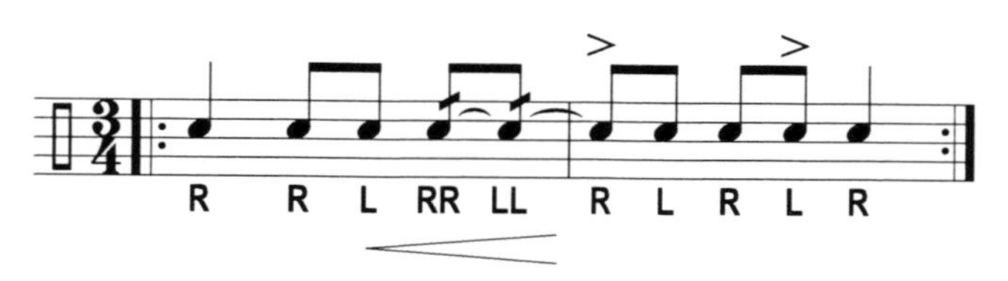

Now, put it all together and you have my primary beat from the chorus of this great song.

Example 9E: Hand and Bass Drum (Chorus 0:48)

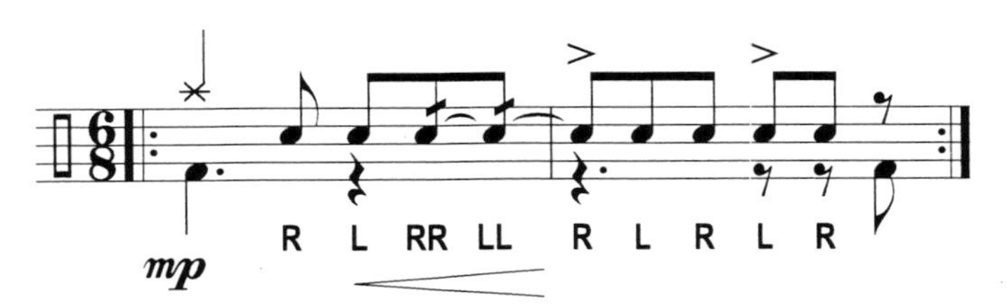

Example 9F: Written in $\frac{3}{4}$

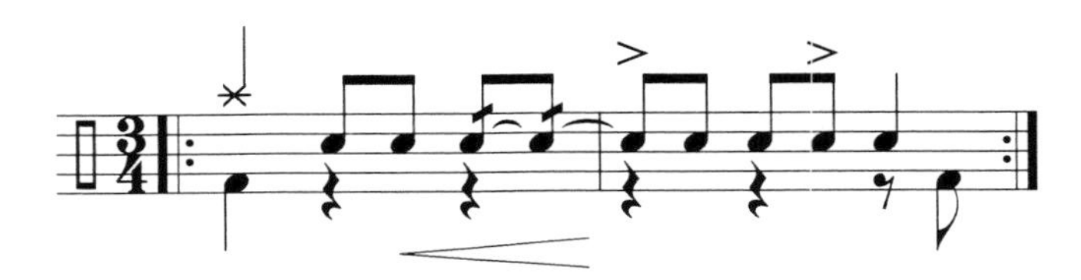

Lastly, let's look at the 2 against 3 feel that's implied in each second measure of the beat. I'll give a few examples of ways I like to practice these cross rhythms. These will all be written in $\frac{3}{4}$. I honestly find it really fun to challenge myself when working on cross rhythms. It's so exhilarating to be able to unlock some bit of coordination among your limbs that you couldn't do when you awoke that morning. Once you've got a cross rhythm down, it's like riding a bike—you might be a little rusty if you haven't played it for a long time, but chances are you'll retain that muscle memory and be able to call upon that coordination forever. As drummers, I feel it really strengthens our inner pulses to understand and be able to play multiple feels and meters at once. Welcome to my head and my idea of fun!

Try these examples in different combinations, for example: A+B, D+H, F+H.

I'd also suggest practicing all of these examples a few different ways, for example:

1. Hands Only
2. Hands and Hi-Hat
3. Hands and Bass Drum
4. Feet Only
5. All Four Limbs

Example 9G: Cross Rhythms

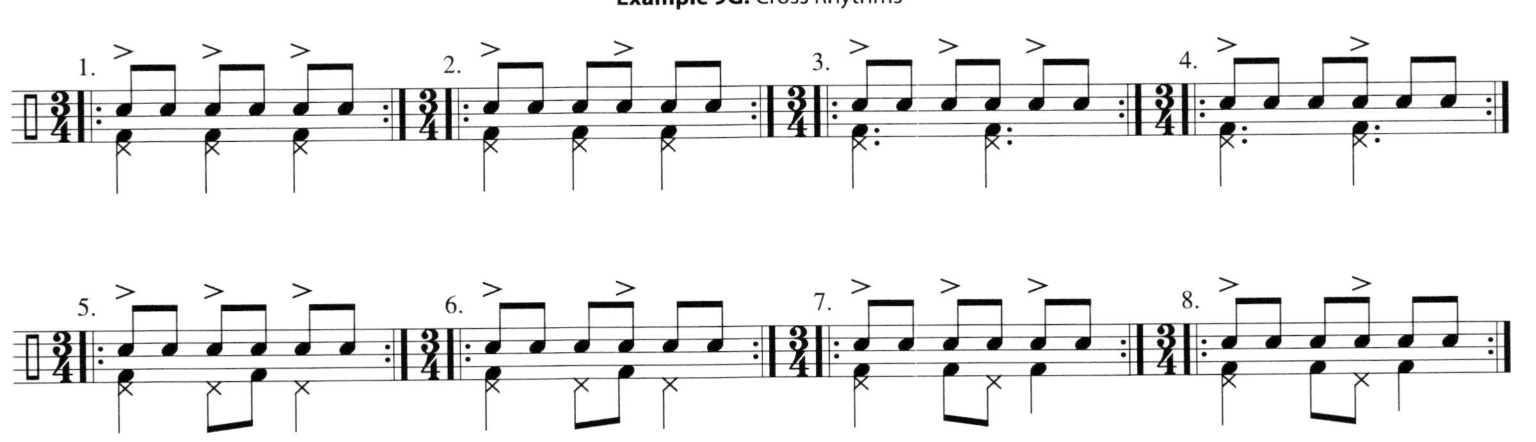

ART OF ALMOST

Wilco from *The Whole Love*

Up until now, the beats have largely been in $\frac{4}{4}$ time with the beat being subdivided in four groups of two eighth notes. This beat is felt differently. The basic clave rhythm, or the way the subdivisions are grouped, is 3+3+2. That is three eighth notes, followed by three eighth notes, followed by two eighth notes. That equals a total of eight eighth notes, or one measure.

The ride pattern generally follows the bass drum part, and the hi-hat openings add a little flavor. I play it with the shoulder of the stick on the edge of the hi-hat in the intro and instrumental sections, and play with the tip of the stick on the top of the hi-hat when the syncopated bass line is present during the verse sections.

Example 10A: Art of Almost

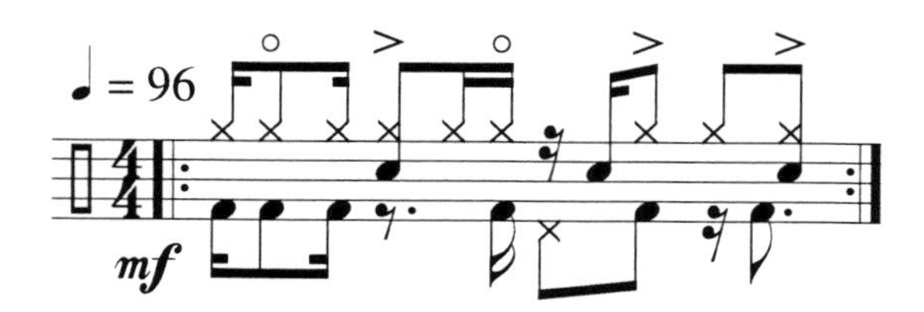

Let's step back and take a look at just the clave. Here is an example of the 3+3+2 grouping.

Example 10B: Clave

Next, just add a basic snare drum and bass drum pattern with straight eighth notes on the hi-hat to better illustrate how this clave works as a groove.

Example 10C: With Snare Drum and Bass Drum, 8ths on Hi-Hat

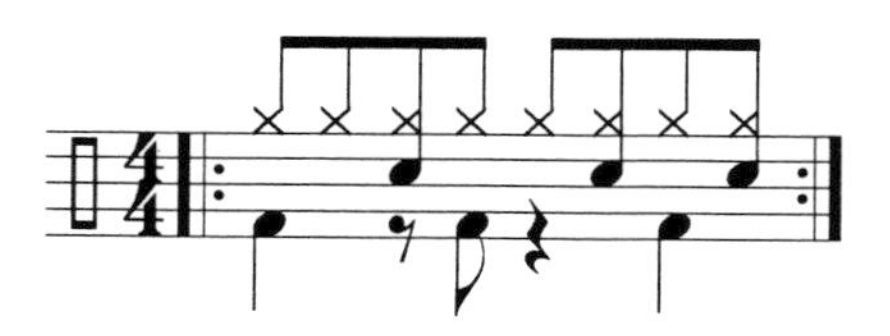

The following example illustrates the snare drum and bass drum punctuations of the "Art of Almost" groove, but with straight eighth notes again on the hi-hat.

Example 10D: Straight 8th on Hi-Hat with "Art" Punctuations

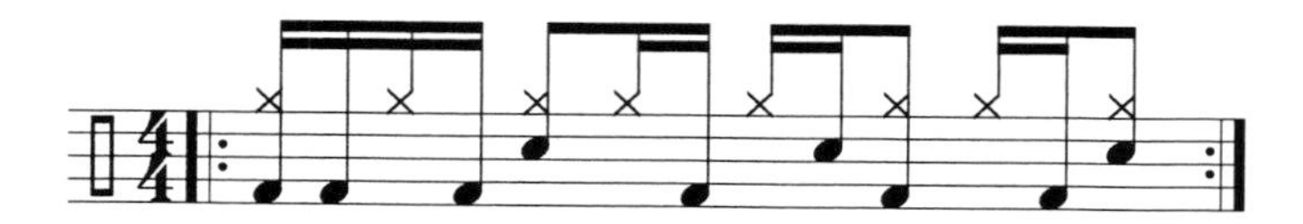

Now if we add the rhythmic hi-hat part, we're just one step away from the actual beat. Notice that the hi-hat remains closed in this example (this is the only difference from the actual beat). This is notated using four groups of two notes instead of the 3+3+2 clave, as it's easier to read in $\frac{4}{4}$ (keep in mind it's still felt as 3+3+2).

Example 10E: Adding the Rhythmic Hi-Hat

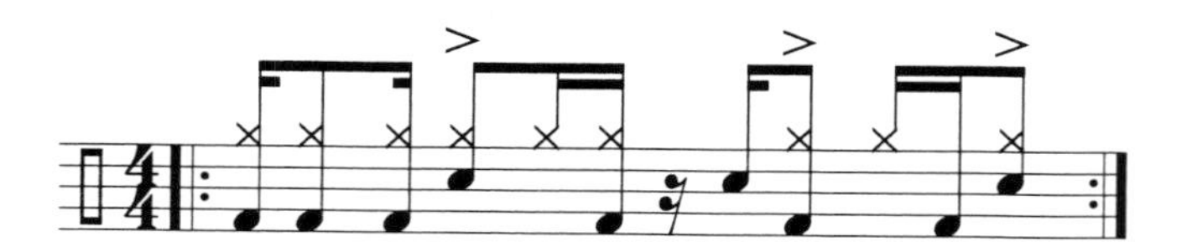

Both for the recording and live, I play around with slight variations on the main beat. These are either added snare drum ghost notes or extra bass drum notes. I throw these in at will. The first variation adds a snare ghost note on the "e" subdivision of count 2, and an extra bass drum note on the "+" subdivision of count 2.

Example 10F: Variation 1

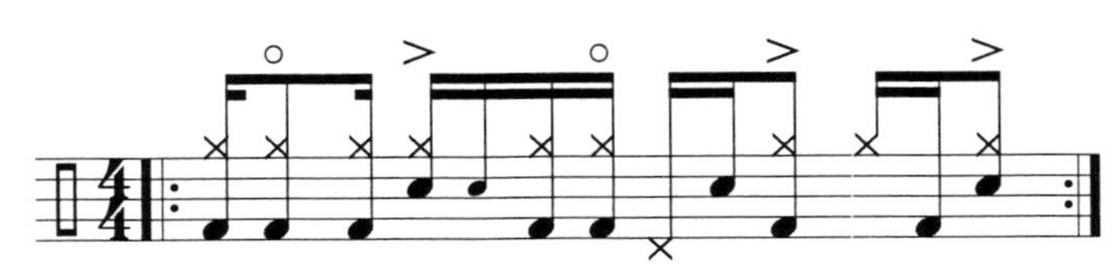

The next variation includes these new additions, adding an extra bass drum note on beat 4, and an extra snare drum ghost note on the "a" subdivision of count4.

Example 10G: Variation 2

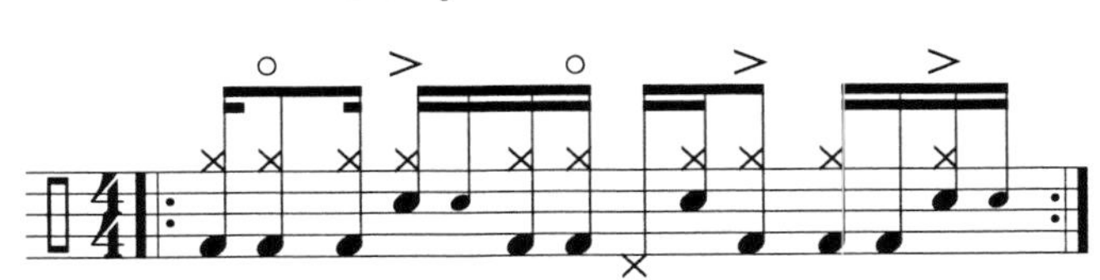

The third variation keeps all the above additions, but adds one more snare drum hit on the "a" subdivision of count 3 as well. This is one I use quite a bit when performing the song live.

Example 10H: Live Version

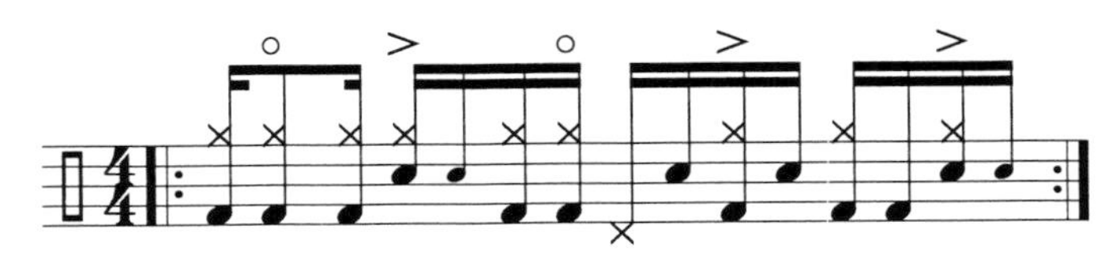

The pad that triggers the three samples (one low tom explosion and two differently pitched reverb punctuations) is on my right side above my floor toms. As a result of my right hand playing the ride cymbal, a little crossover occurs when my left hand comes over to hit the second floor tom in the sample sections.

Example 10I: With Samples (2:08)

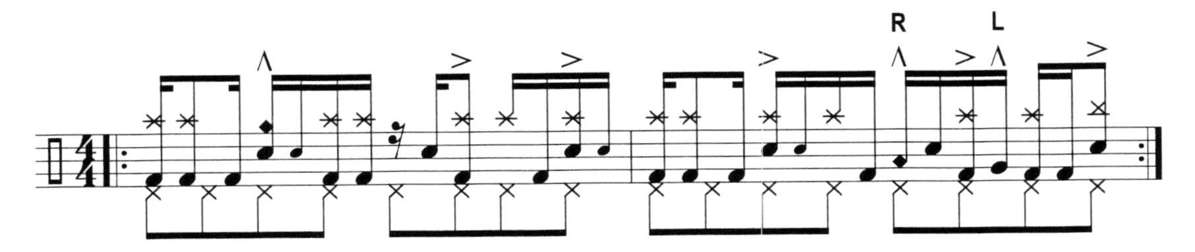

When playing the intro live, I use a stick with small jingle bells fastened to it in order to emulate the prepared kit used on that section for the recorded version. Since this adds considerable weight to the stick, I use multiple-percussion sticks with no taper or bead (basically super thick timbale sticks). Even though I set down the jingle-bell stick after the introduction of the song, I keep using the multi-sticks. I don't find a reason to change to normal sticks since I like the way they sound and feel for this song.

THE LATE GREATS

Wilco from *A Ghost Is Born*

This is a swung, or triplet-feel, beat. The left hand plays a simple half-time back beat part on the snare drum, with an upbeat ride part in the right hand played on the floor tom. Superimposed under this is an implied double-time pattern in the feet. I couldn't decide which feel was best when coming up with the part: the half-time back beat works well with the guitar part but the implied double-time feel gives the groove energy and forward motion. I thought it just made the most sense to play both of them simultaneously.

First, let's look at what the hands are doing. You can see the emphasis on the upbeat floor tom notes on beats 2 and 4. This gives a little funk to the beat and also meshes with the hi-hat part. The back beat on the snare drum is on beat 3, which gives it that half-time feel. The small notes are ghost notes and are optional.

Example 11A: The Late Greats
Hands

Next, let's isolate what the feet are doing. The hi-hat is affixed with two sets of jingle rings, and I play it as loudly as I can (almost stomping on the pedal board). This creates accents on beats 2 and 4, which gives it that implied double-time feel.

Example 11B: Feet

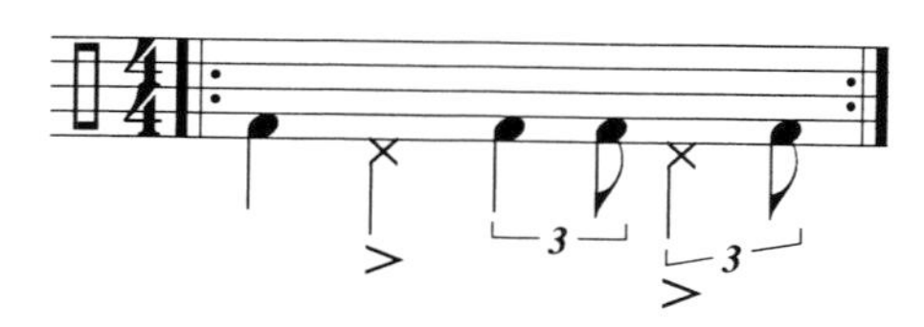

Now, try them together and concentrate on keeping the feel from straightening out. Since the swing feel comes primarily from the bass drum, you'll need to leave enough space and lay back on the two notes on the "a" subdivision on beats 3 and 4.

Example 11C: Combined Hands and Feet

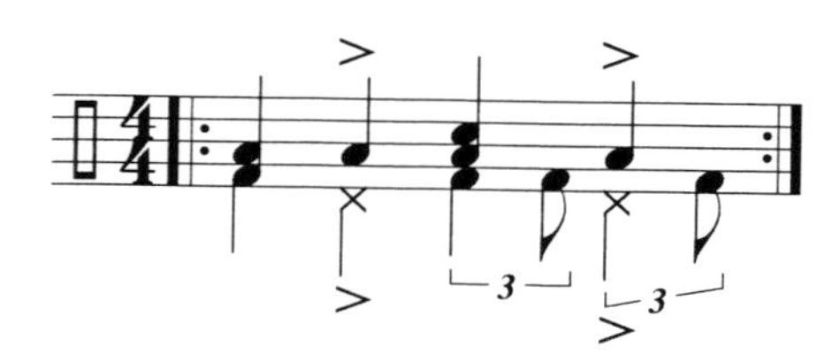

It might be easier for some people to read this beat on two separate staves. This is how it looks.

Example 11D: Separated Hands and Feet

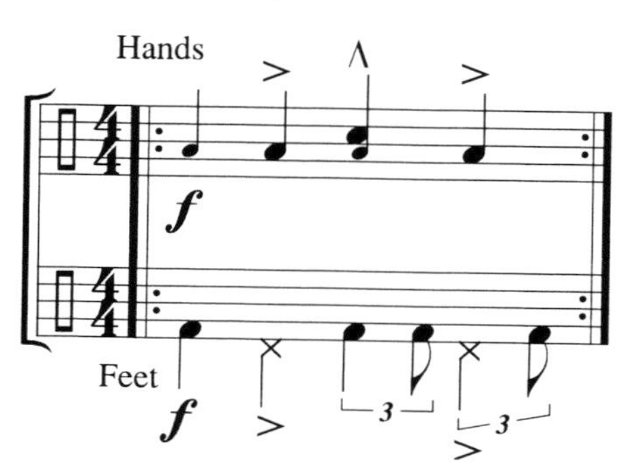

I also like to voice the right-hand ride part between my two floor toms. I typically use 14" and 16" floor toms, tuned approximately to the interval of a major 3rd. I do this when the guitar chords change. This back and forth between the high and low pitched floor toms helps to accentuate the chord progression. I start on the lower floor tom. The asterisks denote when I switch drums.

Example 11E: Floor-Tom Voicings

HEY CHICKEN

Loose Fur from *Born Again in the USA*

This song has quite a few different parts and drum beats. For this week, we're going to concentrate on what I'll call the pre-chorus beat that first appears at 0:27. This part is in $\frac{4}{4}$. However, the accents imply a different or false downbeat. They give the impression that the beat has turned around or shifted. Due to the shape of the guitar line and the accents on the drums, the listener feels the third note in our unison band figures on beats 2 and 4. In actuality, it's on the "+" of 2 and the "+" of 4. Since the third note of the riff is the highest pitched for the guitar and bass (played by Jim O'Rourke and Jeff Tweedy, respectively) and, since I'm accenting that third note, your ear naturally orients to the emphasized note.

Here's how the beat is written.

Example 12A: Hey Chicken (0:27)

The voicings of this beat are a little unusual, but they work. The accent happens on the toms (with the bass drum reinforcing) instead of the snare drum. As a counterbalance to those tom accents, the hands play the snare drum in unison with a slightly opened hi-hat on the "+" of beats 1 and 3.

Here's how our ears are most likely hearing the beat.

Example 12B: Turned Around

The riff is pretty cool this way too, but by shifting everything and putting the emphasis on the upbeats, the whole feel is a little more funky and syncopated, which is more interesting in my opinion.

CHAPTER 4

Beats Incorporating Percussion

WEEK 13

RAIN DROPS KEEP FALLING ON MY HEAD

Jim O'Rourke from *All Kinds of People: Love Burt Bacharach*

This is a tribute record Jim did of all Burt Bacharach songs. I came to Tokyo and recorded most of my parts in a few days. The drums largely came first, with Jim working out many of the arrangements as we went along. He knew what kind of re-working he was going to do with each song as far as the overall tone goes. And, he's always able to lead me in the right direction, but Jim did give me quite a bit of leeway in coming up with specific parts to the songs. The example that I'm choosing here is from the introduction of the song.

In place of a ride pattern, I keep the micro-time (or the subdivisions) with a shaker in my right hand. The shaker part is just steady sixteenth notes.

Example 13A: Raindrops Keep Falling on My Head
Shaker Right Hand

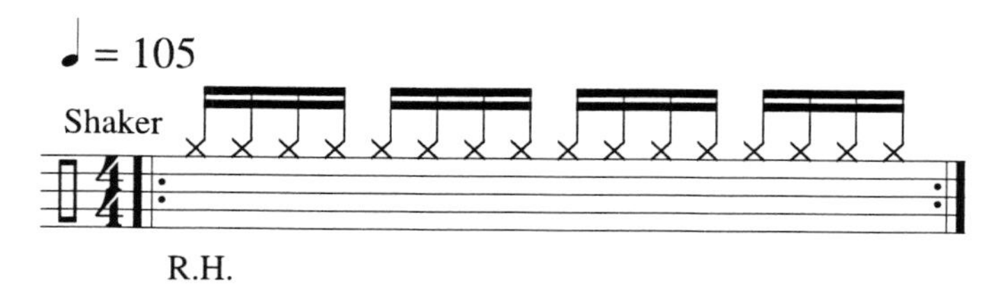

Next, try the shaker with the addition of the bass drum part. The bass drum line stands alone as its own rhythm rather than just one component of a beat. It reminds me a little bit of some of Tony Allen's bass drum lines that seem more like they're an individual rhythmic hook, not necessarily needing the other voices to help it get across.

Example 13B: Shaker and Bass Drum

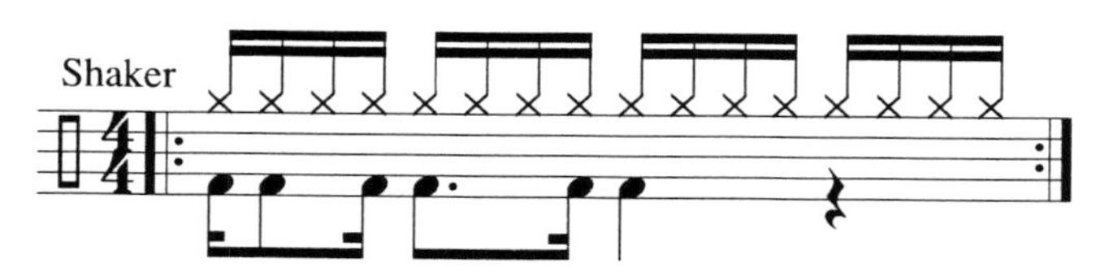

Now let's try the shaker and the other voices. The left hand adds a big half-time back beat on beat 3 and a snare drum cross-stick on the "+" of beat 4 that echoes the hi-hat played with the foot on beat 4.

Example 13C: Shaker and Left Hand

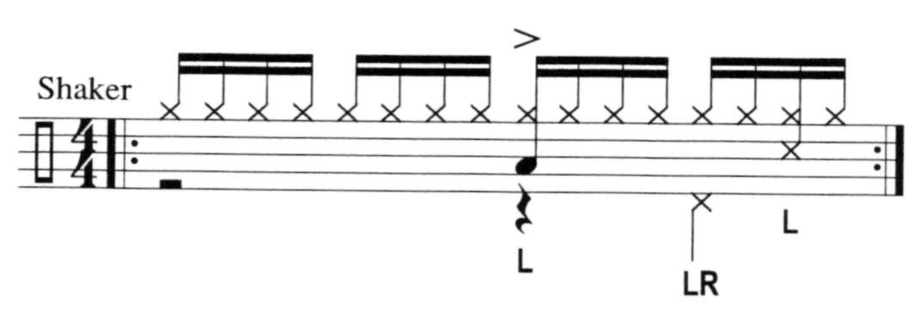

If you put it all together, you get this.

Example 13D: Full Beat

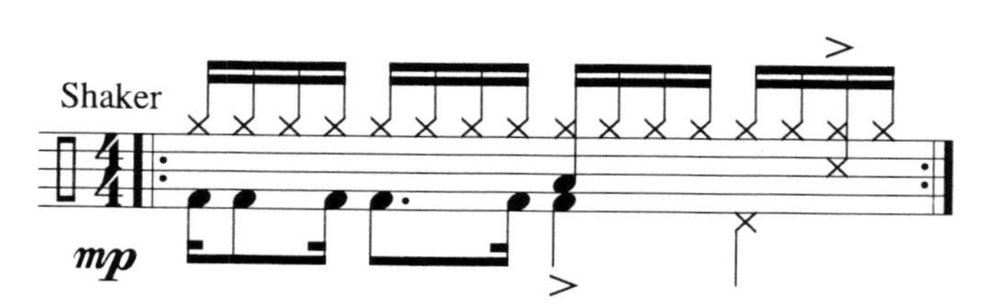

You get a half-time feel by moving the back beat to beat 3 instead of beats 2 and 4. When the rest of the voices are playing rhythms that don't necessarily counterbalance the half-time back beat feel, you can come up with some pretty interesting grooves. There are a lot of reggae beats that have this element to them. There's a back beat on beat 3, but sometimes a driving bass drum or hi-hat quarter-note pulse as well. This is an example of a basic type of reggae beat.

Example 13E: Basic Reggae

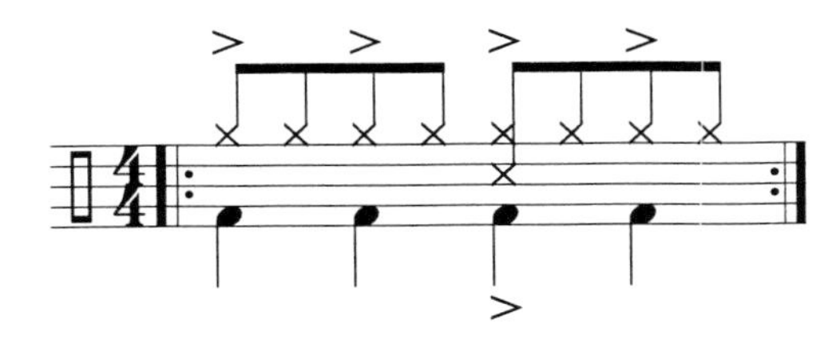

I think learning a variety of reggae beats really helped me to explore alternative back beats when playing around with new beats. As I've stated in other parts of this book, once the fundamentals of all these different types of beats from all styles of music the world over are ingrained in your consciousness, they become assimilated in your drumming vocabulary. And when you need to come up with something fresh or out of the ordinary, you've got all of these resources to draw from. Think of the spark that Jamaican music added to the music of bands like The Police or The Clash. Stewart Copeland and Topper Headon are two of the most creative and driving rock drummers of all time. The more words you know, the better you'll be able to express what you're thinking. The same goes for drumming—the more beats, styles, and the concepts behind them you know, the more versatile and creative you'll be able to be as a drummer and artist. And, the better you'll be able to communicate with other musicians, and convey a piece of music more effectively.

WEEK 14

BULL BLACK NOVA

Wilco from *Wilco (The Album)*

This is one of a few Wilco beats that is highly influenced by German Krautrock. I love this music, and the static, repetitive, and driving drumming really left an indelible mark on me. That music was definitely something I was channeling when coming up with the beat to this song. The beats in the verses remain completely stagnant (in a good way!) except for one factor—the metallic accents on the "+" of count 4 in every other measure. Those sharp and cutting accents go with the narrative of the song and the lyrical content. I play the main beat open handed, meaning my left hand plays the ride part on the closed hi-hat, and my right hand provides the back beat. The bass drum part goes right along with John Stirratt's hypnotic bass line. First, let's just try the basic beat. So this is just the hi-hat, bass drum, and snare drum parts.

Example 14A: Bull Black Nova

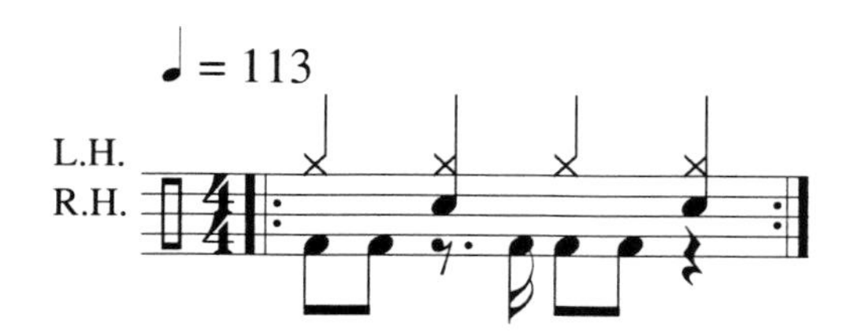

Next, let's add the floor tom on the "+" and "a" subdivisions of count 4 in the first measure of this two-measure beat. This is the answer to the snare back beat on count 4, kind of a response to or echo of it.

Example 14B: Adding the Floor Tom

Now let's take the second bar of the phrase and add the metallic hits on the "+" of count 4 in place of where the floor tom is in the first measure. I play this hit on a variety of sound sources. In the studio I alternated between an LP cowbell, a large mixing bowl with loose snares inside of it, a Gregg Keplinger homemade cymbal, and a Factory Metal Percussion iron cross, which has jingles mounted on it. Live, I still use the FMP but I also use several different types of Zildjian prototype frying pans that my marvelous drum technician, Nathaniel Murphy, mounted on hi-hat clutches. This allows us to just mount them piggyback style on the end of the cymbal stand rod, on top of (but not touching) my cymbals.

Here's what the second measure of the beat looks like.

Example 14C: Adding Metallic Percussion

And finally, let's put the two halves together to get the full beat.

Example 14D: Full Beat

WEEK 15

CARS AND PARTIES

Edith Frost from *Wonder Wonder*

This song was initially a conundrum for me. It's honestly the last time I can remember being truly stumped in coming up with a part for a song. When I got the demos before going into Electrical Audio studios in Chicago with Steve Albini recording the proceedings, I was mapping out some ideas for approaches or parts to songs. I was coming up blank for this one. I remember clearly driving back from an improv gig in St. Louis with Tim Barnes, who I had just played with, along with Darin Gray. The three of us also made up the rhythm section for Jim O'Rourke, with Tim and I double drumming most of the time when I wasn't playing vibraphone. I was playing the Edith demos for him and expressing my trouble in coming up with a good approach to this song. Tim was always a fountain of ideas and suggested I try something from my past—something more like a marching beat.

Since I did spend years playing in marching drum lines, this was the perfect suggestion. I went with a quarter-note pulse in the feet on the bass drum and the hi-hat. And the two of us, throwing around ideas in the car as I drove, came up with the main beat for the song. I play unison rhythms on the snare drum and floor tom while using a maraca as my floor-tom mallet. When I went in for the sole rehearsal before recording began, I remember this beat taking most of the other musicians by surprise. But they were open-minded friends and all receptive to trying it a new way. I do throw in little twists and turns with the rhythm sporadically, but this is the general gist of a four-bar phrase with this type of beat.

Example 15A: Cars and Parties

I think I first got the idea to use a maraca as a stick when writing a percussion ensemble with one of my former teachers, Kevin Lepper. The piece is called "Hunting the Lion," and it's a grade-school level percussion quartet. If I remember correctly, we had a maraca and floor tom part we wanted to play at the same time. Since it's a quartet and the other three players already had parts, we had to be creative. So, Kevin suggested we use the maraca as the mallets for that part. That was an early and important example of thinking creatively, and had a huge impact on the creative development of my playing.

WEEK 16

LAMINATED CAT

Loose Fur from *Loose Fur*

This is still one of my favorite beats to play. It's basically two overlapping beats. When I play it live, the first one begins the song, and the second joins in after the first chorus. First, let's look at them separately. This song begins as a kind of psychedelic drone piece with Jeff Tweedy's lyrics and voice floating on top of a bed of amorphous goodness (care of Jim O'Rourke). I knew I wanted to play something static and that didn't have any baggage attached (meaning a beat that people wouldn't immediately associate with another type of song).

The bass drum part goes right along with Jeff's vocal phrasing, where his initial lines pause on the "+" subdivision of count 2. I didn't want the back beat to be too intrusive so I turned off the snares. A standard 2 and 4 back beat didn't feel that great and when I tried playing double hits on the back beat (adding in the "+" of beats 2 and 4) it felt too sing-songy and vintage rock 'n' roll glee for this particular song. But, when those double hits are shifted forward to occur on the "+" of count 1 and the "+" of count 3, it feels right. They were out of the way of the bass drum as well, and hence the vocals. Perfect! In place of a ride pattern, I shake a couple of smaller sheep bells I taped together and hold horizontally like a standard shaker. That clicking really blended well with the other percussive timbres and was more staccato than a typical shaker. As a result, it took up less sonic real estate too—all good things, in my opinion. I keep a steady quarter-note pulse on the hi-hat, which has one of my homemade shakers attached to it to ground everything.

Let's learn this beat progressively to make sure everything is locked-in before we add the additional part from the second verse. Let's start with the snare drum and bass drum. The following examples are from the live arrangement of the drum part.

Example 16A: Laminated Cat (approx. 0:10)

Next, let's take the feet along with the shaker/right-hand part.

Example 16B: Bell Shaker Part with Feet

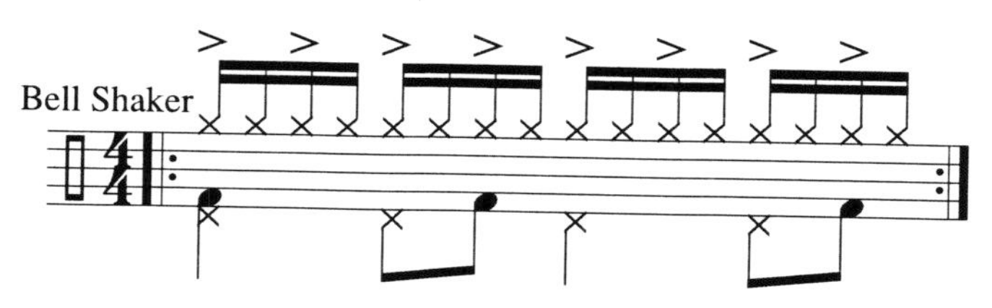

And when all of the voices are in, it looks like this.

Example 16C: First Verse Beat

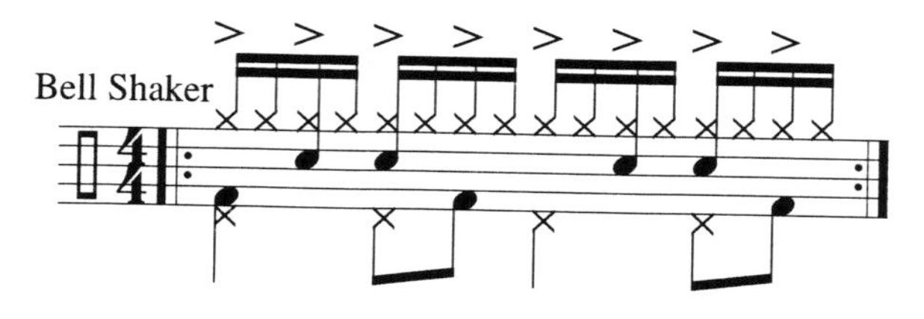

As I mentioned, a new voice appears after the first chorus. In order to do this live, I set my bell shaker down on the last lyric of the chorus so it's not missed. That means I have the four-bar transition between the chorus and the second verse to set the bells down, pick up a maraca and reset the beat. I use the maraca as the mallet in my right hand as I did in "Cars and Parties" from Week 15. I play a counter rhythm with it on the toms. Which tom I use depends on what chord the band is playing. I have three toms I switch between every time a chord changes in the progression.

For the sake of space, I'll just write the floor tom line here, and let you experiment with moving it around and voicing it as you please.

Example 16D: Floor Tom Accents with Maraca

I'm not very strict about whether I only play these accents or whether I fill in some of the other eighth notes. I don't feel it adversely affects the character of the beat by adding them in.

Example 16E: With Inner Beats

It can be challenging to play all of these elements together so, once again, let's take it progressively. Let's start slowly with just the hands.

Example 16F: Hands Only

Next, try just the right hand and the feet. Notice that the floor tom accents are aligned with the first two bass drum notes but not the third. That one will align with the snare drum. If you can get those associations right, you've got the beat.

Example 16G: Right Hand and Feet

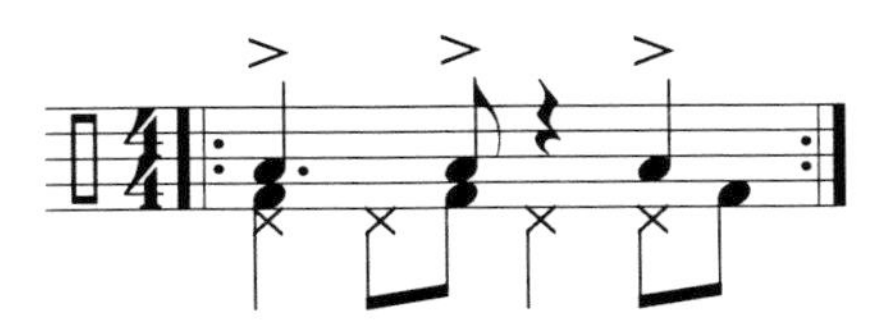

Finally, let's put it all together.

Example 16H: Second Verse Beat (approx. 2:01)

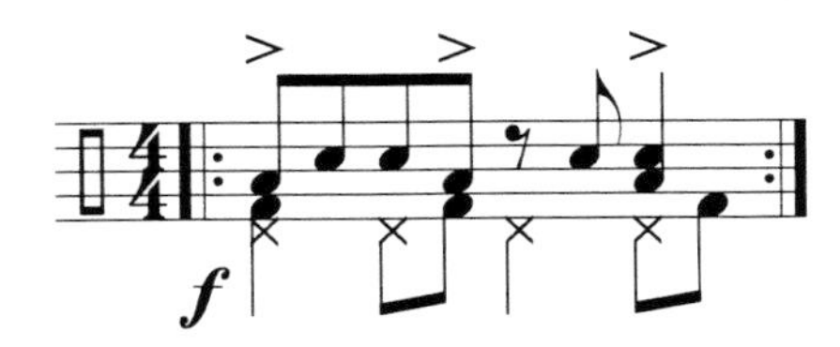

Earlier, I mentioned the homemade shaker I attach to the hi-hat stand for this beat. That's something that I use quite a bit. I originally used an array of egg shakers fastened to two metal rods that were tightened between the felts of a hi-hat clutch. I can use these independently by loosening the hi-hats so only the shakers sound, or in tandem with the hi-hats. I wrote an article for *Modern Drummer* magazine explaining how to make these (part of a series of articles I wrote called "DIY Percussion," available on my website). Latin Percussion later took this same idea and turned it into their Chick-Ita Hi-Hat shakers as well.

CHAPTER 5

Beats with Unconventional Hi-Hat Use

WEEK 17

DEADLIGHTS

birddog from *Ghost of the Season*

For this week, we're taking the beat from the chorus, which is closely related to the other beats in the song. At the top of the song, I'm riding on the rim of the snare drum with a bamboo multi-rod. I also keep time alternating between two little metal measuring cups I have overturned and resting on a pad on top of the snare head. For the chorus, I move the time to the ride cymbal and play a straight back beat on the snare drum, also with a bamboo rod hitting a piece of fabric I have on the snare head. The only thing out of the ordinary is that I split up the bass drum counter balance to the back beat (typically falling on and around beats 1 and 3) between the hi-hat and bass drum. Let's take the hands with only the bass drum first.

Example 17A: Dead Lights
Hands and Right Foot

Now let's take the hands with the hi-hat/left foot part.

Example 17B: Hands and Left Foot

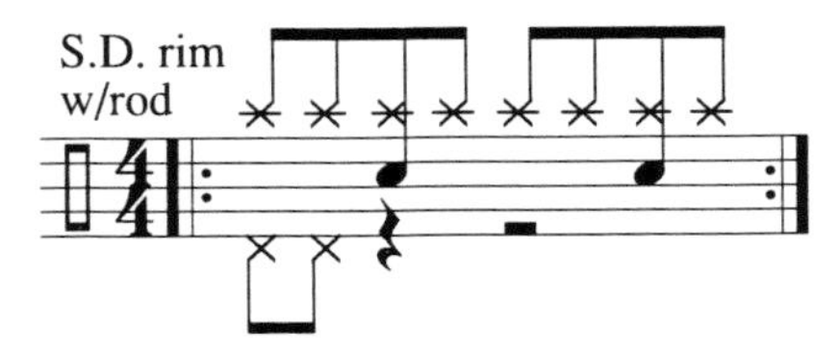

And with all limbs together, we have this.

Example 17C: Full Beat (0:46)

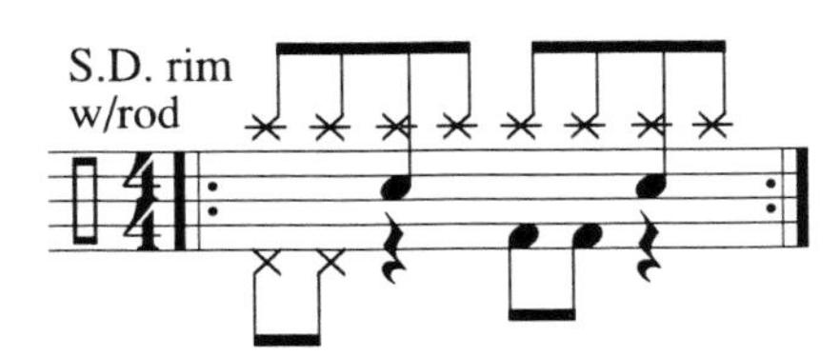

Occasionally I'll throw in some other bass drum notes at the end of phrases that act as light fills so as not to disrupt the flow of the beat.

Example 17D: Bass Drum Variation

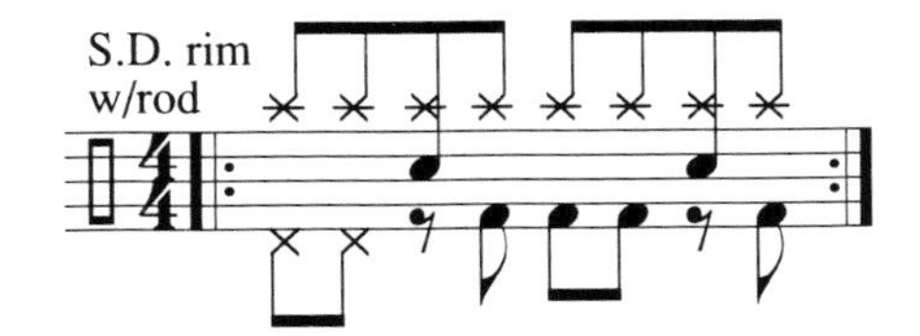

CARNIVAL KNOWLEDGE

Loose Fur from *Loose Fur*

This is the beat from the introduction of the song. A variation of it also appears in a few spots throughout, substituting a tom run for some of the sixteenths played on the hi-hat. This intro beat has only two voices, the hi-hat and the bass drum. The hi-hat is more like a snare drum part with the openings taking the place of a press roll. I change the opening of the hi-hats around throughout, so here are a few examples.

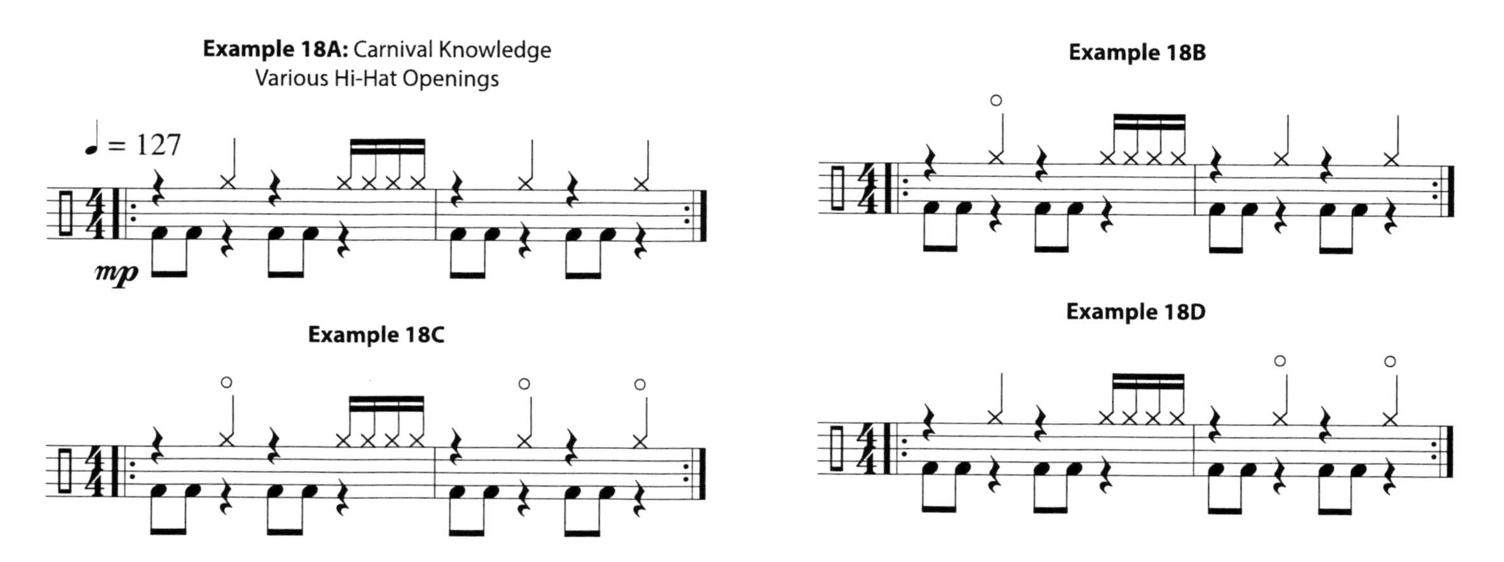

These are all very simple beats. And, simplicity is often the best place to start. If it works, like this beat did, then great. Now you have something that already works but can be easily embellished when the part re-occurs later in the song. And, that's exactly what I did. Here's an example of the first variation. It has the addition of a snare drum back beat.

Example 18E: Adding a Snare Back Beat (0:43)

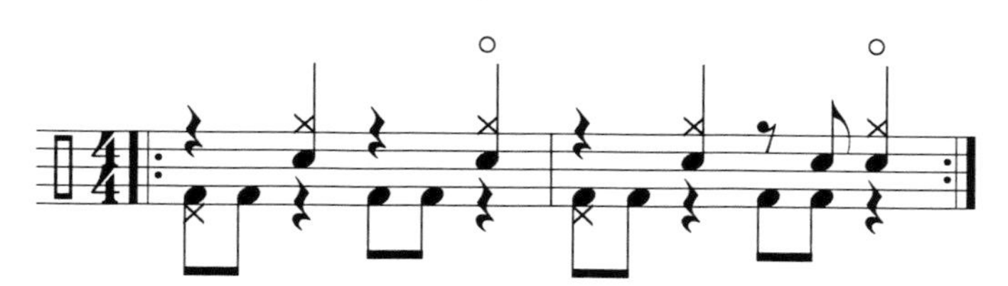

For the next variation, a tom run is substituted for the sixteenth notes on the hi-hat.

Example 18F: Tom Run in Place of Hi-Hat 16ths (1:10)

One little quirk I love about this variation is that the cymbal crash is solo. Rarely does a cymbal crash sound right without the support of a bass drum or snare drum underneath. Since this isn't a typical beat, it doesn't feel empty to have the crash sounding alone. If there was more of a consistent kick / snare beat happening, this might not work as well.

WEEK 19

I MIGHT

Wilco from *The Whole Love*

This is a stripped down beat with one small twist. The main feel comes from the driving guitar part. I felt like a simple, yet aggressive quarter-note snare beat (similar to the many faster, driving Motown hits) would best heighten that feel. I didn't want it to be too metronomic though, so I added the upbeat bass drum part as counterpoint. The hands are just laying down the time with unison quarter notes on the snare drum, and my right hand on the floor tom instead of hi-hat. Here are the hands only.

Example 19A: I Might (Verse)
Hands Only

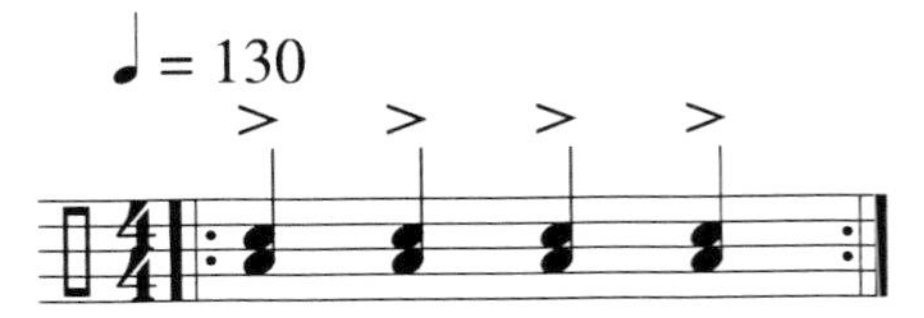

And here it is with the bass drum as well.

Example 19B: Hands and Bass Drum

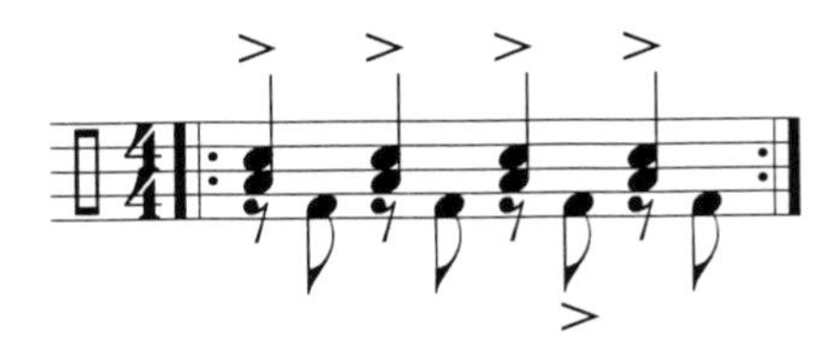

Hearing the back beat on all four beats made me think of "Satisfaction," by The Rolling Stones, which has that same beat. In turn, that made me think about the distinctive tambourine part in that song, with its strong accents on counts 1, 2, 3, the "+" of 3, and 4. I thought I might pay a little tribute and overdub that very part. As we rehearsed the song in the studio though, I began to experiment with playing that rhythm with my left foot on the hi-hat, loaded with jingle attachments. It proved a bit challenging at first, but came together by the time we started tracking the song. Since the addition of the left foot hi-hat part is deceptively tricky, I've broken it down here to learn in conjunction with the other individual elements of the beat. First, let's just try the left foot part alone.

Example 19C: Hi-Hat Only

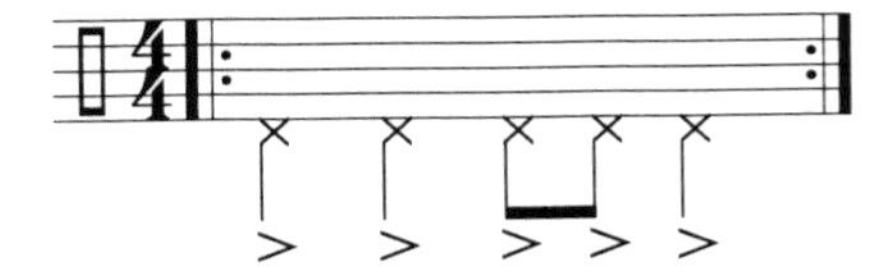

Next, let's add the hands.

Example 19D: Hands and Hi-Hat

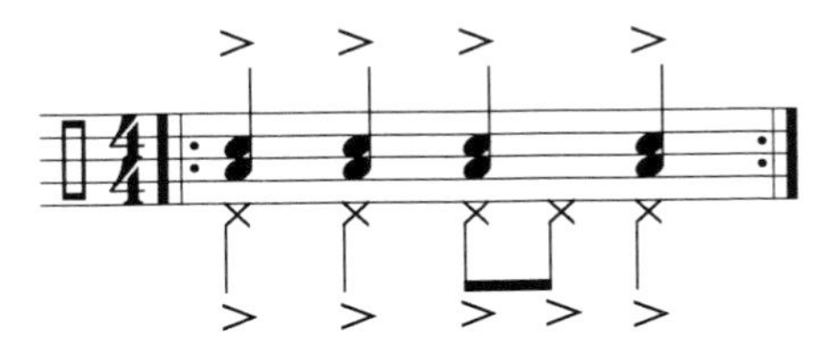

Now, let's try the feet together keeping in mind that the "+" of count 3 will be the toughest part, since both feet play together on that subdivision instead of alternating left, right, left, etc.

Example 19E: Feet

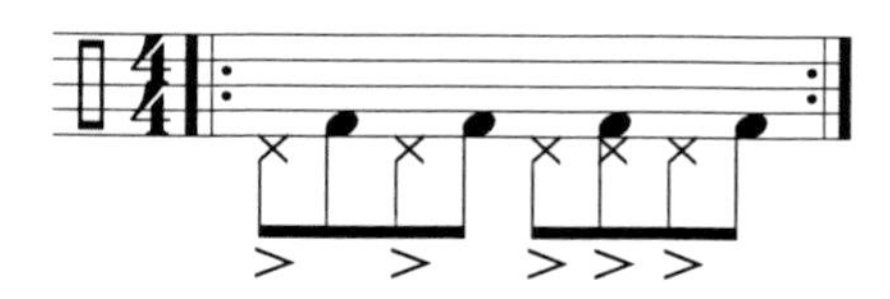

When learning this part, I found it's helpful to some people to actually say the stickings out loud while practicing the part. Therefore, one would say, "left, right, left, right, left, both, left, right."

Finally, let's put all the pieces together. Make sure you really play the left foot part with force and conviction so it matches the volume and intensity of the other three voices.

Example 19F: Main Beat

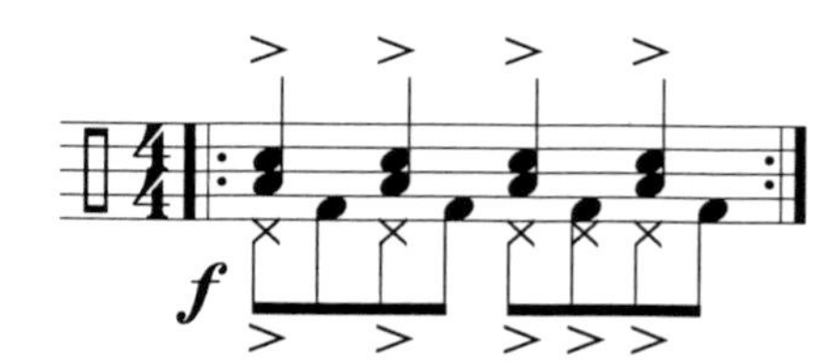

EXTRAS:

Once you've got the beat nailed down and solid, I've included three examples of snare fills to try. The first one I use quite a bit, throwing it in wherever I feel it from night to night. It's just a little sixteenth-note tag on the very end of the groove. The second one adds a little double hit on the back beat towards the end of the phrase. And, the third example is something fairly exposed I play during the final verse where the rest of the music is stripped down a little bit. It kind of answers the guitar part at that spot.

Example 19G: Fill Ex. 1

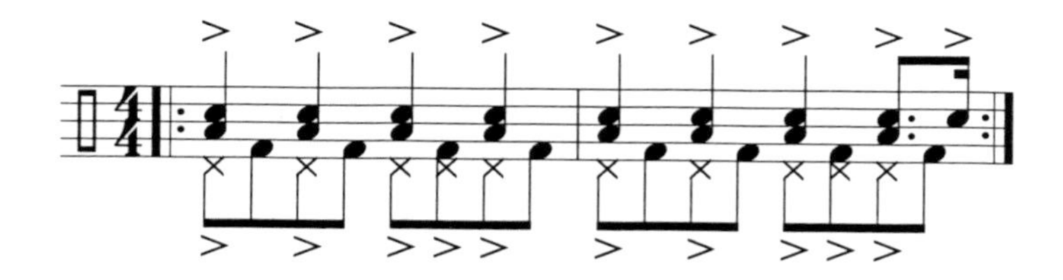

Example 19H: Fill Ex. 2

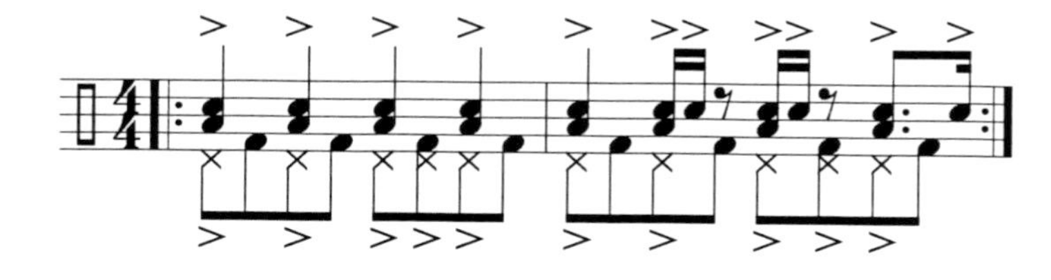

Example 19I: Fill Ex. 3

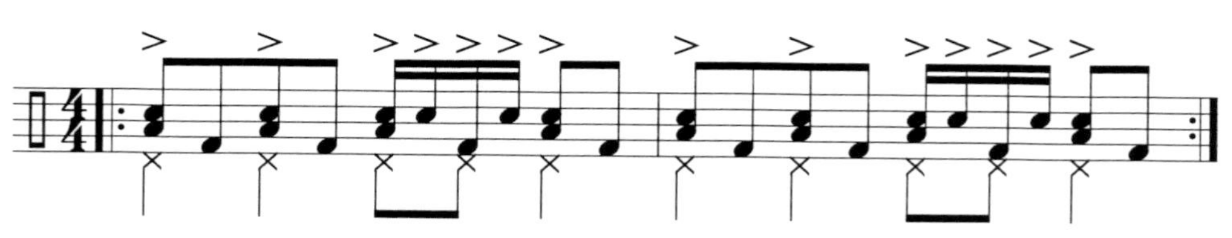

WEEK 20

ANOMALY, MVT. 4

Kronos Quartet with Glenn Kotche from *Adventureland*

In 2006, Kronos Quartet commissioned me to write a piece for string quartet with drumset. I ended up writing a seven-movement work that required the quartet to not only play their instruments in a traditional manner, but to also use percussion and extended techniques as well. I too was required to play a wide breadth of percussion and techniques. The kit included a glockenspiel and crotales, Earth plates, a cocktail kick, snare and toms, woodblocks, bell cymbals, and noisemakers such as LP Crickets, hand bells, and little friction drums. Even though I wrote most of the piece starting on the drums and then orchestrating for string quartet, the beat that follows is one of the few that appears in the work. This is mainly due to most of my parts being just that—parts, instead of repetitive beats.

This one comes at the culmination of an emotional movement and occurs at one of the high intensity points of the piece. I use the hi-hat as a kind of alternate snare drum with rhythmic figures being traded between the two voices. That interplay between the snare and hi-hat is the focal point of the beat. Since the strings are winding down at this point, the drums have more of a featured role rather than the supportive one while this beat is being played. Therefore, it's a bit more busy and dense than most of the beats in this book. The rolls switch between duple and triple bases as well. I remember studying snare drum with Ken Snoeck and working from Anthony J. Cirone's *Portraits in Rhythm* book. Ken had me really think about the base of a roll, which is the rhythm of the roll and how to use that as a tool, but also how to mask it so the rolls are smooth and void of pulsing. Let's start with just looking at the underlying rhythm and leaving out all of the decorative notes. Keep in mind that the first four bars simply repeat with one minor change between the fourth measure and the eighth measure. There's one additional bar at the end to make this a nine-bar phrase. But measures 1–3 are identical to measures 5–7.

Example 20A: Anomaly, Mvt. 4
Stripped Down

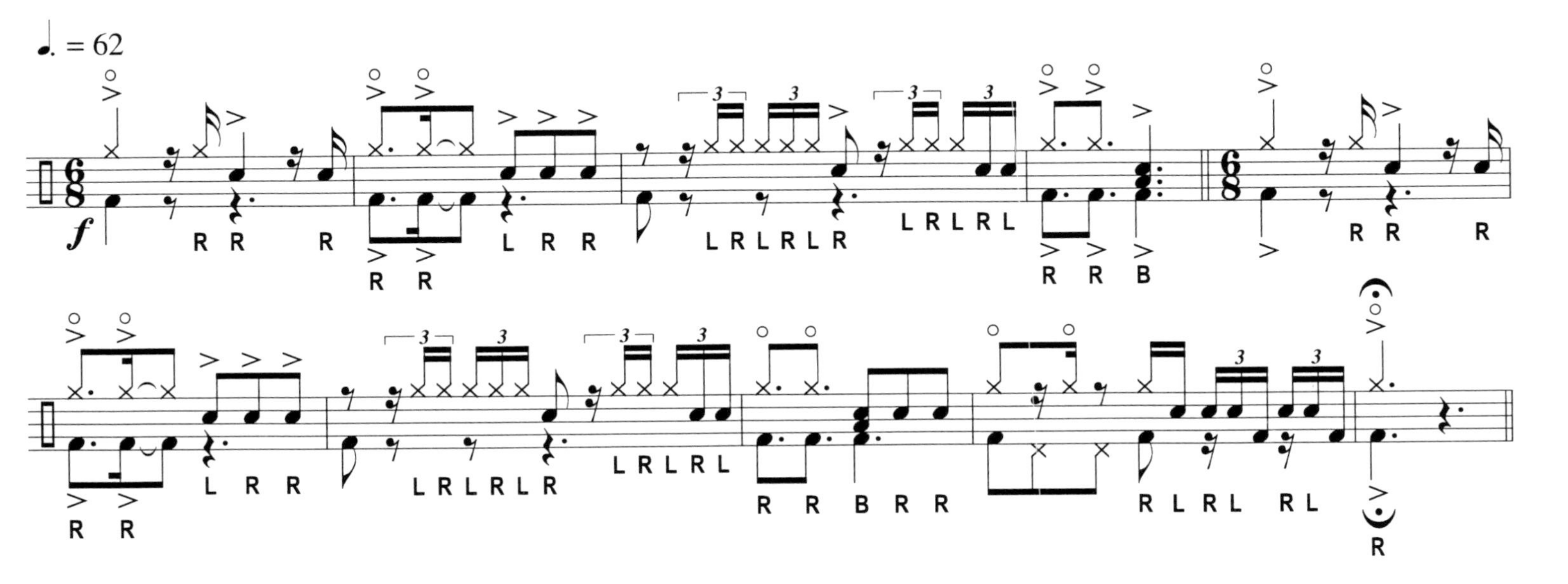

Instead of breaking this one down piece by piece, I think diving in might be the best plan of attack. Again, just dissect it one measure or one beat at a time, and then start to string the pieces together.

Example 20B: Full Beat (2:22)

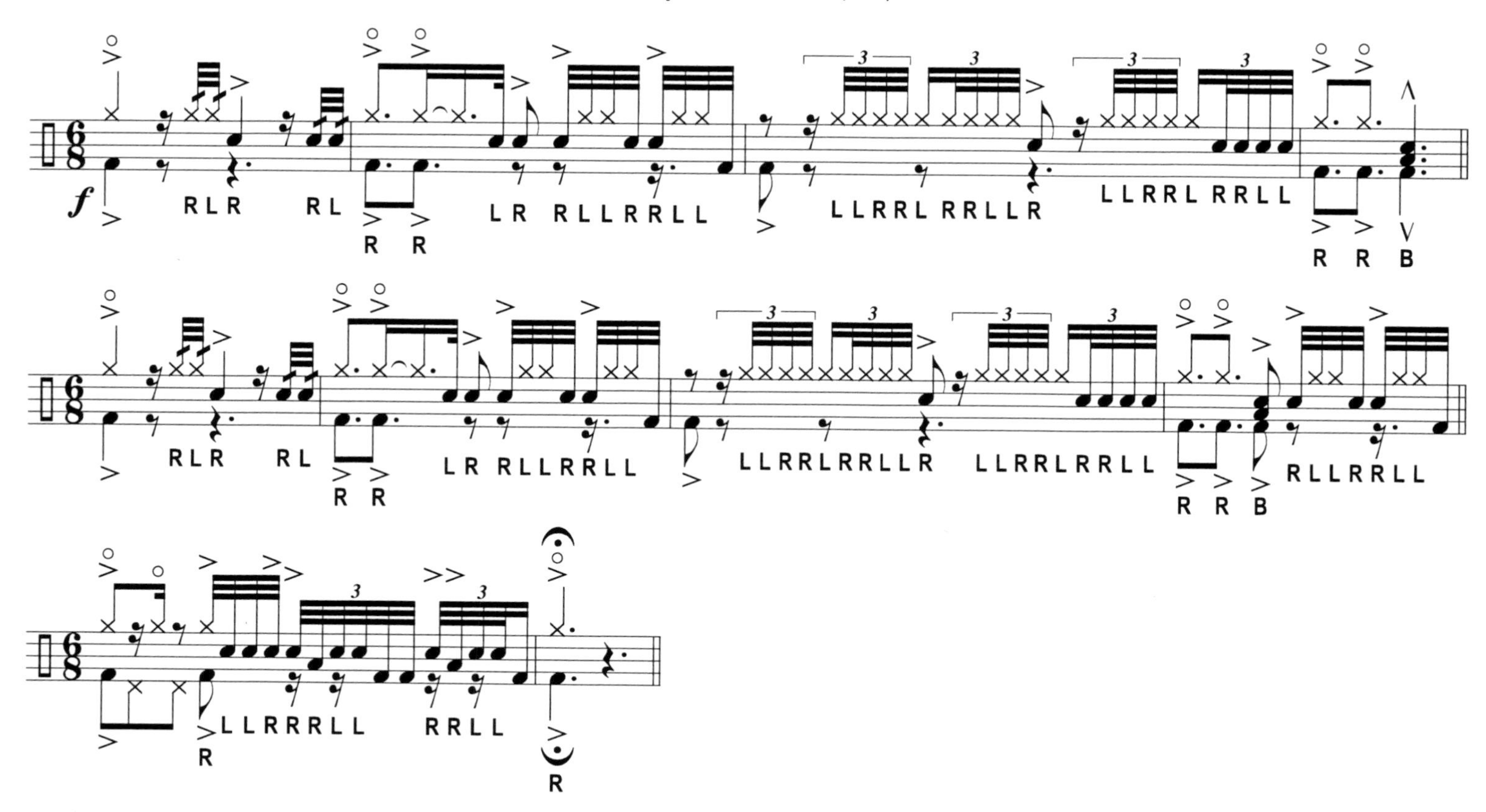

CHAPTER 6

Pattern Beats

THE TIES THAT BIND US

7 Worlds Collide from *The Sun Came Out*

When I was asked to be a part of Neil Finn's 7 Worlds Collide project, I was thrilled at the prospect of making music with some of my heroes. One of those is Phil Selway, drummer and founding member of Radiohead. Very unlike my song contribution to the project—a percussion duet of sorts, composed from Radiohead and Wilco drum parts—Phil's contributions caught everyone by surprise. He brought in two beautiful, gentle acoustic guitar-based folk songs. He was singing and doing some fantastic fingerpicking parts on the guitar. As his song, "The Ties That Bind Us," started coming together, much to my surprise, he asked if I heard any drum parts that I might want to add. I knew that a traditional drum part would ruin the flowing feel and gentle character of the song. Instead, I opted for playing more of a graduated pulse part in the verses and a pattern groove in the choruses.

If I had to define what I'm calling a pattern groove, I'd say that it's a beat that's linear in nature and more akin to a melodic line than a traditional rock groove. I usually reserve this term for linear grooves or lines that incorporate several different musical timbres, and require a series of moves on different parts of the drumset that, when all put together, become a really interesting composite beat.

I had done some things like this in my past, but the inspiration came from a source that Phil wasn't too familiar with. I remember Craig Belford, a fellow high school drum section friend of mine, playing a Jethro Tull song for me and both of us marveling at how the arrangement was comprised of a series of instrumental (many of which were percussion) textures that were layered on top of each other as the song progressed. The song is called "Skating Away on the Thin Ice of a New Day," and the effect of the percussion and overall arrangement is brilliant. The song keeps evolving and increasing in excitement in no small part because of the percussion. I decided this was the best approach for Phil's song.

I save the groove for the chorus when the song peaks, waiting until the lyric is mostly done and adding a kind of answer to it that sounds every other measure. The lyric starts on beat 2 with the last syllable on the "+" of count 3 in the next measure. I play on that last syllable and continue with eighth notes on various surfaces until the following count 2, when the lyric enters again. I decided (with Phil's blessing, of course) on varied percussion timbres, including two different pitched tambourine hits, a cymbal scrape with a pastry knife, a cymbal bell hit, and two different tom pitches. I leave the feet out entirely for this one.

I found this part most easily played live by holding four implements. I use the Musser grip, which I learned when studying four-mallet marimba. This grip offers more independence than the other popular four-mallet Burton grip—which I also utilize quite a bit—but sacrifices a bit of power for that independence. Since this song is relatively quiet, power isn't an issue and, since I am playing on several surfaces, independence is a great asset. When I studied percussion in college under Jim Campbell at the University of Kentucky, he would have me use both grips for multiple percussion pieces depending on what worked best for the performance and sound requirements of a given piece. I strongly recommend that drummers get at least a cursory knowledge of both grips, even if they may never play a keyboard percussion instrument. Having a basic comfort level with both grips may end up solving some complicated drumming challenges you may face down the road.

I ended up using a flat spatula/pastry knife as my outside left-hand mallet and a felt general timpani mallet as the inside left mallet. For the right hand, I used another general timpani mallet inside and a drumstick on the outside. This allowed me to hit the first two tambourine notes with the shaft or mallet head of the right inside mallet, with the left outside pastry knife scraping the cymbal on my left for the third note in the sequence. I then used the outside right-hand stick to hit the cymbal bell on my right side, with the following two tom-tom pitches being played by my left-outside and right-inside mallets, respectively. The text in the following example alternates between the surface and the sticking to best illustrate the performance of this pattern groove.

Example 21A: The Ties That Bind Us (Chorus 1:17)

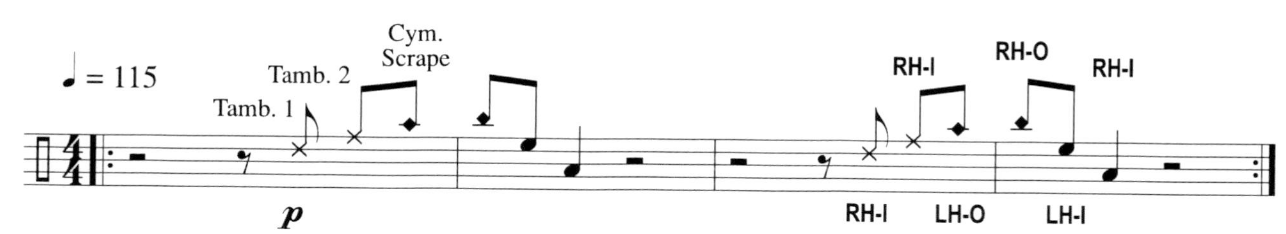

WEEK 22

DEEPER DOWN

Wilco from *Wilco (The Album)*

Like a vast majority of high-school aged drummers in the '80s, I was a big fan of Neil Peart and Rush. Mr. Peart had a lot of interesting approaches to coming up with parts that left an indelible mark on many of us. One of these was his broken paradiddle pattern on the ride-cymbal bell. Another was his choice to often offer a contrast in odd-time sections by playing through them with a straight back beat. Another is the way he constructed pattern beats. One example that stands out is the Rush song "Mystic Rhythms."

When it came to composing a drum part for the song "Deeper Down," I knew that I wanted my parts to reflect the episodic nature of the song structure. This meant a sonic scene change for each verse of the song. I wanted the chorus parts to be a bit more grounded, something I wouldn't change from chorus to chorus. Since there are no lyrics in the choruses, I didn't necessarily have to provide any sort of static rhythm part to support them. A pattern beat was the obvious choice to me.

For this groove, the hands are alternating with the bass drum, which is basically a bossa nova bass drum part. There'll be more about the bossa nova later in Week 41. The bass drum part for "Deeper Down" goes like this.

Example 22A: Deeper Down (Chorus 1:06)
Bass Drum Only

I use regular drumsticks for this pattern beat since no un-traditional sounds are called for. The beat begins with two different bell-cymbal strikes, and then moves to a rhythm that's split up between the floor and rack toms. The second measure of this beat then moves to the hi-hat. The first two hi-hat notes are closed, and played with the tip of the stick on top of the top cymbal. The third note is an open hi-hat played on the edge of the cymbals with the shoulder of the stick. Later, in the second measure, there are three more closed hi-hat notes that resolve with another floor tom hit.

Example 22B: Full Beat

After four measures of this beat, or two repetitions, the beat alternates with a kind of fill beat. This beat is played mostly on the snare drum with the last figure moving to the hi-hat. It has a bit more energy and less space, and works perfectly as a *fill measure*. This beat makes me think of Hal Blaine's playing on some of the Beach Boys records.

Example 22C: End of Phrase Beat

ONE WING (verse)

Wilco from *Wilco (The Album)*

My drum parts for this song are very episodic and change with every new verse or chorus. This two-measure beat pattern happens during the second verse. It's a spacious beat that has its own type of clave. Let's dissect this beat and see what it's made of. Here it is in its entirety first.

Example 23A: One Wing (Verse 1:03)

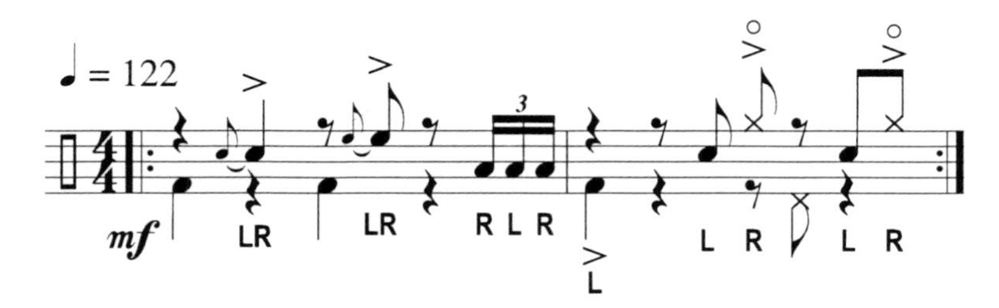

Now, let's strip away everything except the accented notes that make up the primary musical shape to the beat.

Example 23B: Rhythmic Core

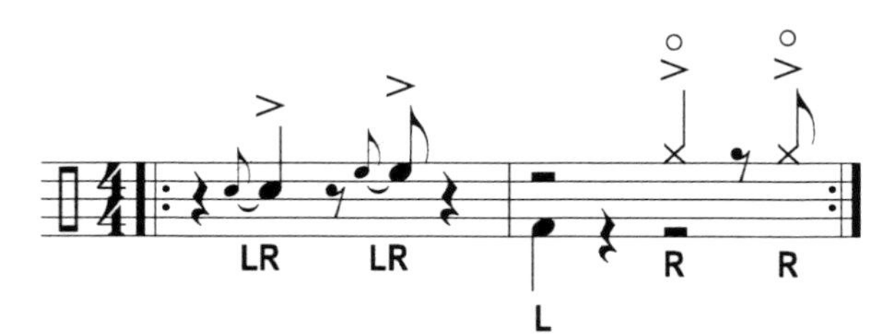

If we shift all of those accents over one beat, we end up with example 23C. This might look familiar to several people working out of this book, as it's the clave pattern for a bossa nova. For this "One Wing" beat, there's a bossa nova clave but just shifted ahead one full beat. A clave pattern is basically the underlying rhythm that the beat and music are based off. I'll have more on that in Week 41.

Example 23C: Clave

Next, let's look at the second measure of the beat. Starting on the "+" of count 2, there's a three-note pattern that's played twice. This gives a 2 against 3 feel. Here is a basic 2 against 3 polyrhythm played between the snare drum and bass drum.

Example 23D: 2 Against 3

Here's the part written as groups of three in the $\frac{6}{8}$ time signature. It's easy to see the three-note grouping when written this way.

Example 23E: Three-Note Grouping

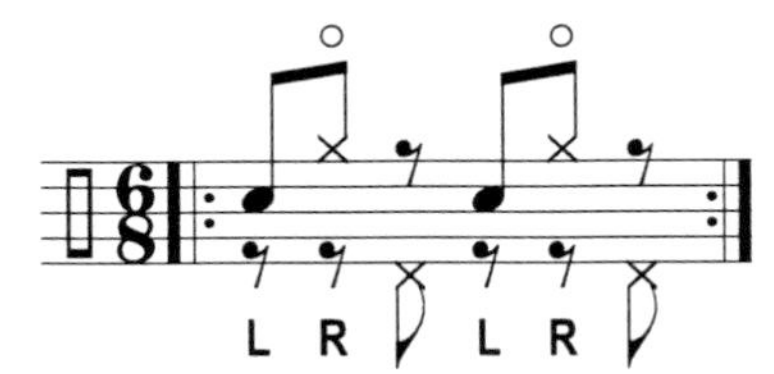

And, here's the same thing written in $\frac{3}{4}$ so that you can see that the contour of the phrase doesn't line up with the three downbeat subdivisions of the $\frac{3}{4}$ time signature as it did when written in $\frac{6}{8}$ time.

Example 23F: Written in $\frac{3}{4}$

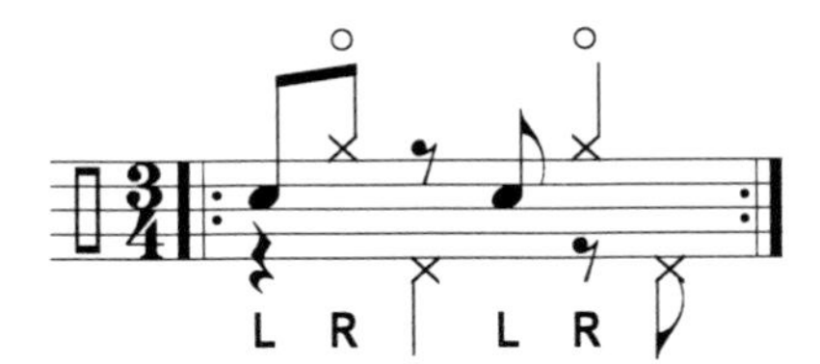

GREAT ESCAPE

birddog from *Ghost of the Season*

This is from birddog's second record and it's an example of a simple pattern beat. It retains a linear line but on a limited number of surfaces. Let's first look at the fully realized beat that happens around 2:22 in the song.

Example 24A: The Great Escape (1:04)

Next, let's look at a more refined version which appears earlier in the song during the second verse.

Example 24B

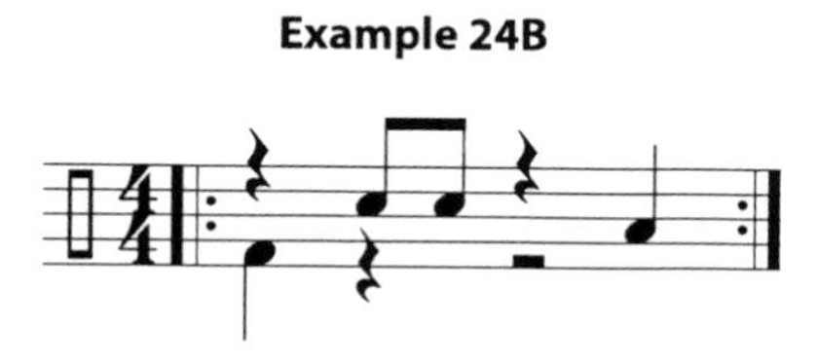

In both of these examples, you can see that the back beat on count 4 is played on the floor tom (with a nylon rod/stick) instead of the snare drum. This simple change of color creates a shape to the part, just as melodic phrases have a shape. The bass drum lands on count 1, which solidifies the groove. The snare back beat then sets up what could be a normal rock beat. By having a second back beat (beat 4) on the floor tom, the entire mood of the beat is darkened and softened. This creates a downward line of pitch from snare to floor tom to bass drum with the rhythm stripped to the bare essentials.

CHAPTER 7

Beats in $\frac{3}{4}$ Time

WEEK 25

WHAT I DON'T BELIEVE

The Minus 5 from *Down With Wilco*

There's something about the song and its playful elements, changing feels, and affected vocals that have always resonated with me. This is the groove from the bridge section of the song. The preceding verse is much more of a traditional waltz feel, with snare drum press rolls and a swung feel. For the bridge, I chose to straighten out the feel as a contrast, which is kind of what the bridge is all about anyway.

This beat might sound a bit odd or complex, but it's actually very straightforward and part of most drummers' vocabulary.

First, let's try the actual beat.

Example 25A: What I Don't Believe (1:15)
Full Beat

Now, let's break it down to just the right hand and right foot. You can see the bass remains constant on the upbeats, and the right hand just moves from two hi-hat notes to the floor tom on count 3.

Example 25B: Right Half of the Body

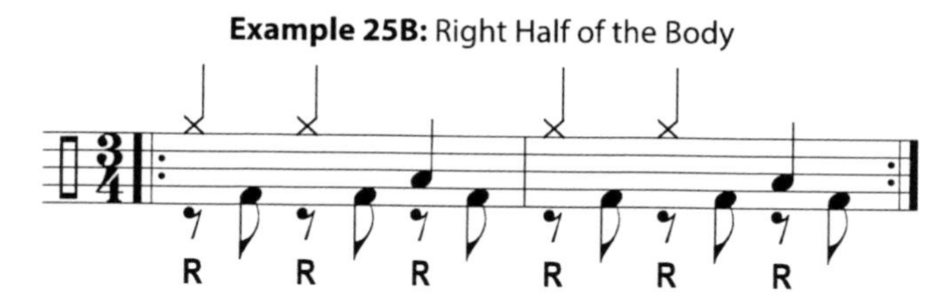

Next, just try what the hands are playing. First, play on one surface (the snare drum), and then with the proper voicings of the beat. Notice that in Ex. 25C, on count 2, we have double-stops and not flams. These need to remain tight in Ex. 25D so they don't dilute the driving aspect of the beat. And, keep in mind that your right hand will be switching back and forth between the hi-hat and floor tom in Ex. 25D.

Example 25C: Hands Only on Same Surface

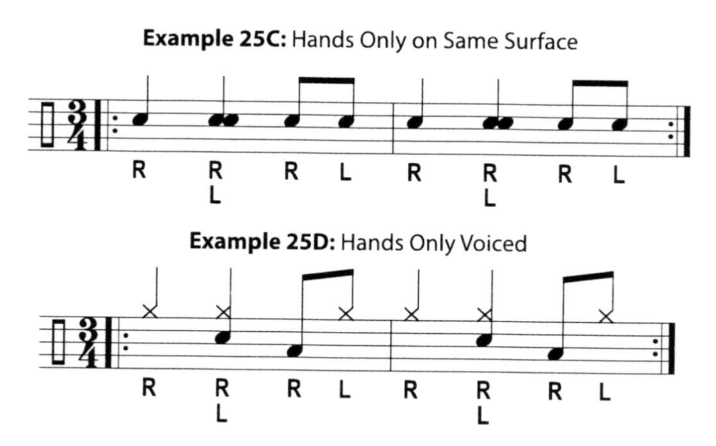

The trickiest part of this groove will be the "+" of count 3. This is the only time the right foot isn't alone. Again, make sure the left hand isn't flamming with the bass drum but is perfectly locked in with it.

Example 25E: Bass Drum and Left Hand

If you can play Ex. 25E solidly, this beat will pose no problems for you.

ALL COMEDIANS SUFFER

7 Worlds Collide from *The Sun Came Out*

This is another song from the 7 Worlds Collide benefit record organized by Neil Finn. On this song, which is Neil's, I needed to provide a super, solid driving beat. I ended up digging pretty hard because the song really rocks and I got into it! I'll go over a few of the various incarnations of the main groove. All are very similar with only subtle changes thrown in as fills or to inject a bit more momentum as the song builds. The main verse beat goes like this:

Example 26A: All Comedians Suffer
Main Beat

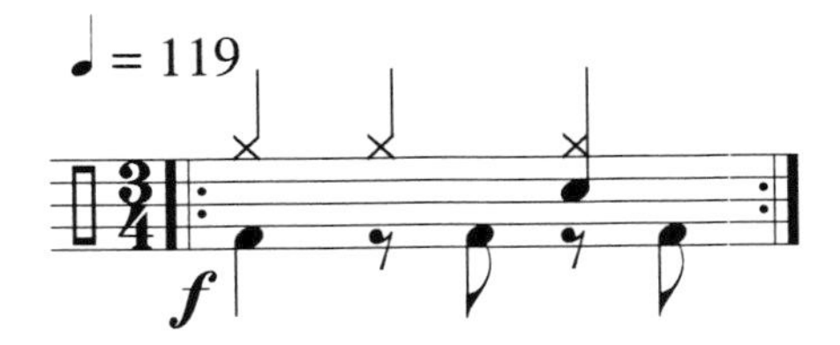

I add an extra snare note at the end of the beat as a sort of fill that doesn't disrupt the flow.

Example 26B: Fill (1:07)

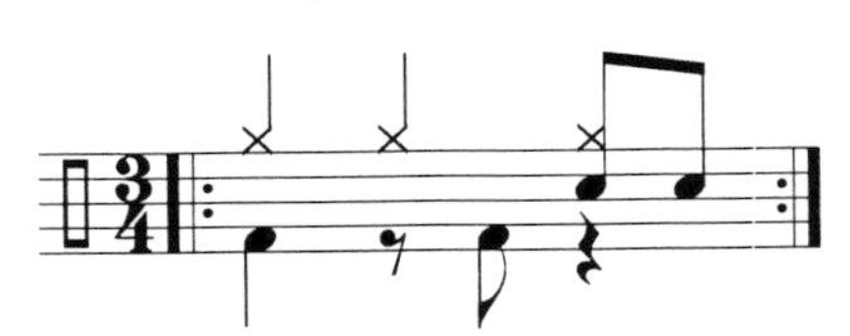

The song changes about mid-way through and ups the urgency. More drive is required from the drums here, so the hi-hat part switches from quarter notes to eighth notes. The bass drum also changes slightly by articulating beat 2 a bit more forcefully.

Example 26C: More Driving Variation

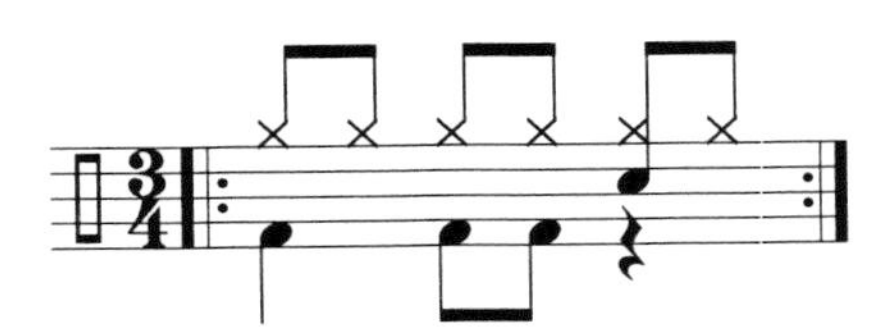

The fill variation of this beat adds a second snare drum note, as does the original verse beat. However, since this section is more driving, the additional snare note happens on the "+" of count 2 (preceding the back beat). I find this little variation gives slightly more forward momentum than if it was on the "+" of count 3 like it is in the verse beat.

Example 26D: Variation Fill (1:56)

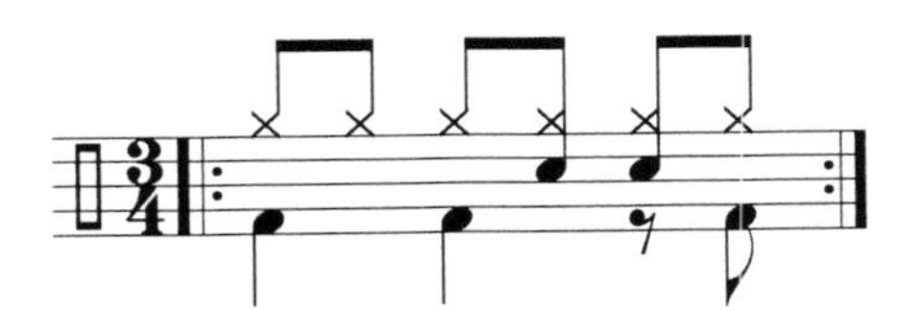

I think it's important to note that I'm keeping a driving eighth-note feel throughout on the bass drum as well. Most of these notes aren't actually even played. I might just be bouncing my right foot lightly enough so the beater doesn't even strike the head, but sometimes it does, adding a ghost bass drum note. I'm fond of this, as it's subtle enough to not disrupt the groove. Occasionally you'll hear an extra note, such as the very top of this song in the solo drums intro. But like ghost notes on the snare drum, it tends to just solidify the groove. In all of my years of training, I never came across bass drum ghost notes, and so I was intrigued as to why this was. As a result, when the tempo and the feel are right, I'll explore the concept and bounce my foot to help keep time which results in bass drum ghost notes. Here's an example of one that occurs in the intro of "All Comedians Suffer."

Example 26E: With Bass Drum Ghost Notes

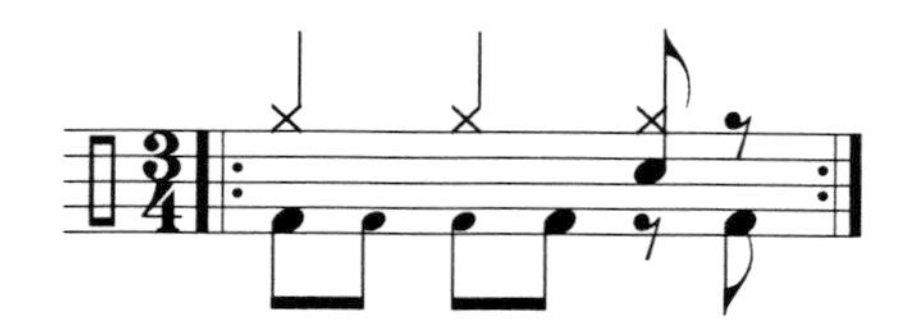

INSIGNIFICANCE

Jim O'Rourke from *Insignificance*

The secret to this beat is all in the feel. It's not complex at first glance, but the complexity is in the exact placement of the inner beats or ghost notes on the snare drum. These notes are swung, but not overtly, as they remain pretty tight and snug to the beat as opposed to lying way back.

Example 27A: Insignifigance
Full Beat (0:28)

As in the previous beat, I find it helpful to try both hands on one surface to make sure everything is falling into place correctly. The small noteheads here depict the ghost notes.

Example 27B: Hands Only on One Surface

SIDE WITH THE SEEDS

Wilco from *Sky Blue Sky*

On the verses of this song, I play a more traditional half-time $\frac{6}{8}$ feel, but change it up to a waltz feel in $\frac{3}{4}$ time on the choruses. For this week, I'd like to focus on the beat from just the chorus sections. Instead of a standard waltz with the snare accent or back beat on count 3 or counts 2 and 3, I place the snare accents on both counts 1 and 3 to match the rhythm guitar part that's happening under Nels Cline's blistering guitar lines. Let's begin with the individual components of the groove. First, let's start with the hands.

Example 28A: Side With the Seeds
Hands Only on One Surface

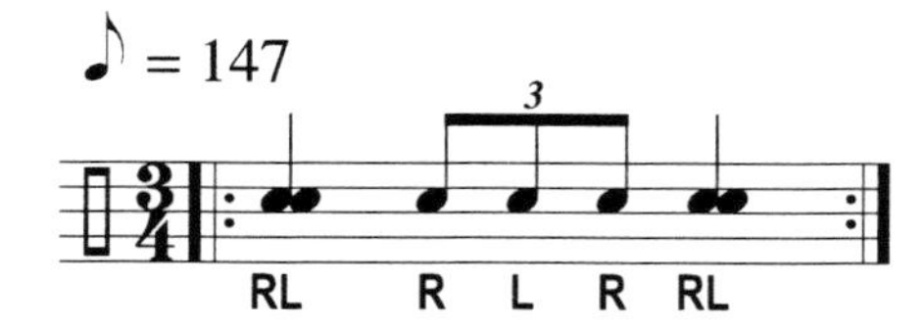

Now, try each combination of limbs to make sure everything locks in correctly. In this next example, you can see that the bass drum is playing all upbeats on the third subdivision of the triplet against a pretty standard swung $\frac{3}{4}$ ride pattern.

Example 28B: Cymbal and Bass Drum

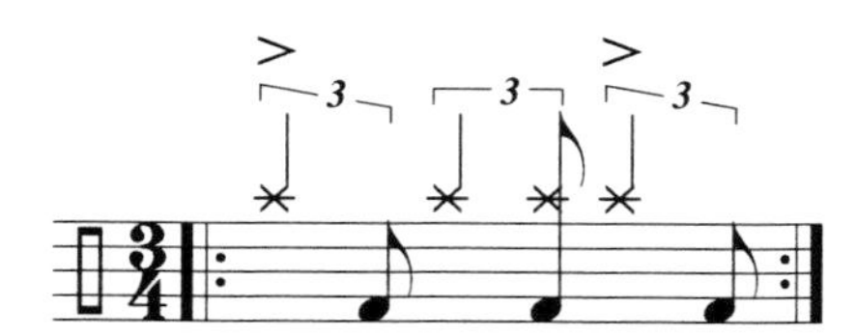

Next, let's just try the ride cymbal and hi-hat parts. The hi-hat is the anchor in the beat for me. That one note keeps me grounded when performing it. Sonically it's the least important note in the beat but, without it, the beat is a house of cards!

Example 28C: Cymbal and Hi-Hat

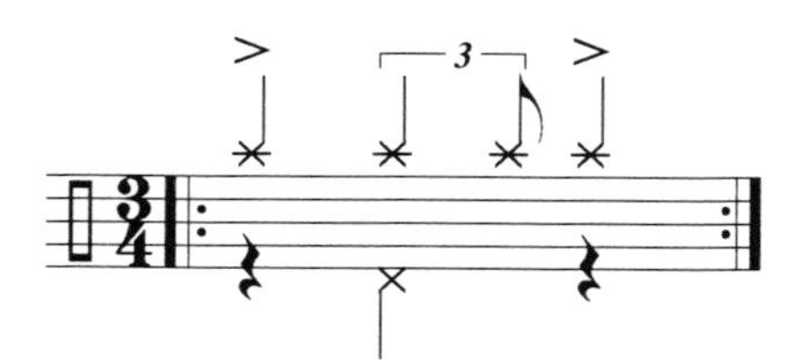

Now, do the same thing but add the snare drum as well. Note that the snare is accented on counts 1 and 3. The middle snare note on the "a" of beat 2 can either be played more like a ghost (or supportive) note or accented, as well as almost a kind of fill occasionally. I play it both ways live.

Example 28D: Cymbal, Snare Drum, and Hi-Hat

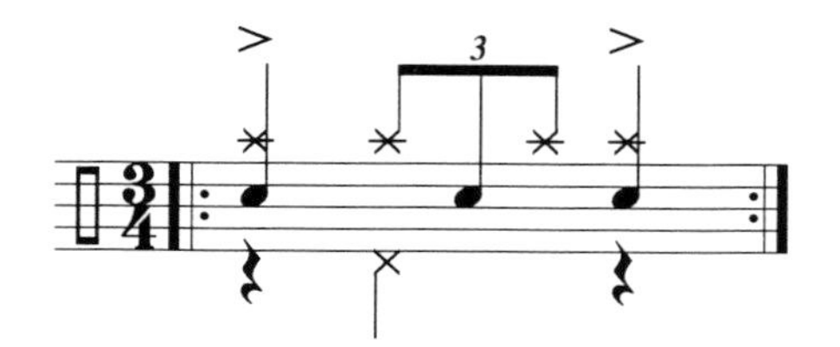

Now, try all the components in concert.

Example 28E: Full Beat (1:49)

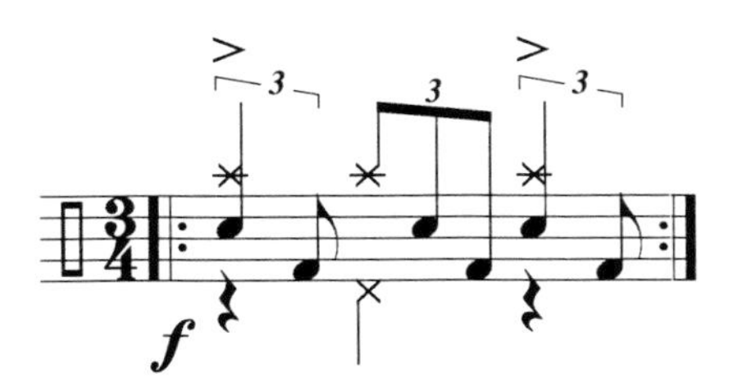

You can see it's very similar to a more common groove. The only real exception is that the first snare and bass drum notes are swapped. Here's an example of this beat's more common cousin.

Example 28F: Close Relative

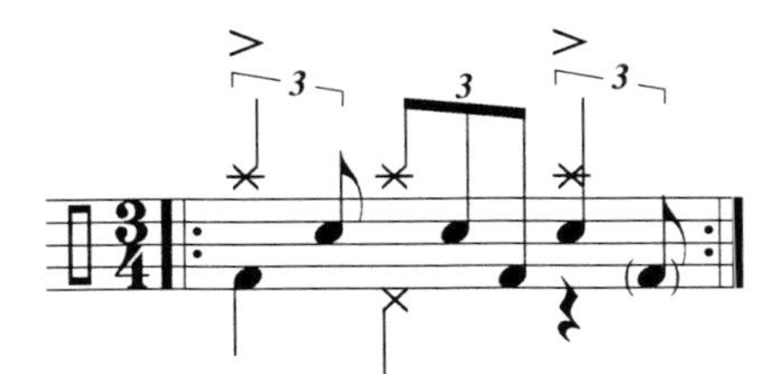

CHAPTER 8

Beats in Odd Times

POOR PLACES

Wilco from *Yankee Hotel Foxtrot*

This example from "Poor Places" is the ending drum part. I play several different types of beats throughout this song, but the ending beat is the most distinctive. I remember clearly being at the mixing stage of this song at Soma studios in Chicago with Jim O'Rourke and Jeff Tweedy. Jim thought the song needed something else at the end, so he asked me to go into the tracking room and play something "march-like, but not too straight and predictable." So with his direction, I came up with this beat in $\frac{5}{4}$ time.

Example 29A: Poor Places
Ending (3:02)

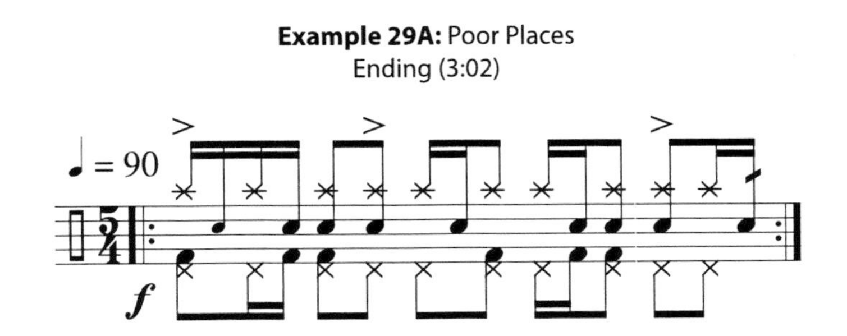

I interpreted "march-like" a couple of ways. First, I thought of the obvious by throwing some type of snare rolls or drags in there. Second, after spending years in the marching bands at Roselle Middle School (under the masterful direction of Bob Wis), the über competitive marching band at Lake Park High School, and eventually marching with the Cavalier's Drum & Bugle Corps, I knew I couldn't think too linearly. When the snare, tenor, and bass drum line play together in a marching percussion section, it's not always a constant trade-off or game of musical tag. Many times all of those subsections are also playing in unison and supporting one another's lines. So, I knew I had to think outside of a normal drumset beat where oftentimes the snare and bass drum are alternating or trading off (which ultimately creates the back beat). Instead, I decided to play a lot of double stops or unisons between the two voices. This sound has a bit more impact and power.

Check out just the snare and bass drum parts together to get a sense of this. Note that the trickiest part will be getting both sets of the consecutive unison sixteenth notes (counts "a" of 1, count 2, and count 4, "e" of 4, and "+" of 4) locked in and avoiding flamming between the two voices.

Example 29B: Snare Drum and Bass Drum

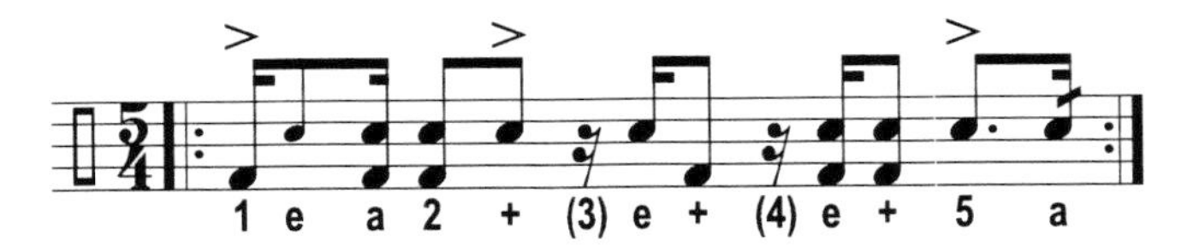

Now try the same thing, but with the hi-hat part (left foot) thrown in.

Example 29C

1 e + a 2 + (3) e + (4) e + 5 + a

Getting those unisons will actually be easier if you play each voice separately with the ride cymbal part, since it's keeping a steady eighth-note pulse in this beat.

Example 29D: Cymbal and Bass Drum

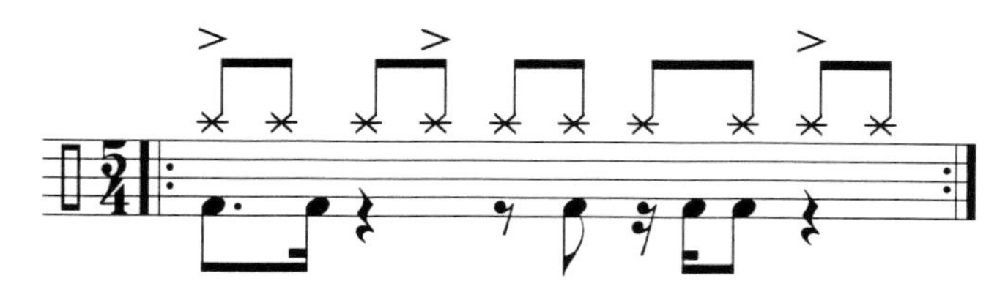

Example 29E: Cymbal and Snare Drum

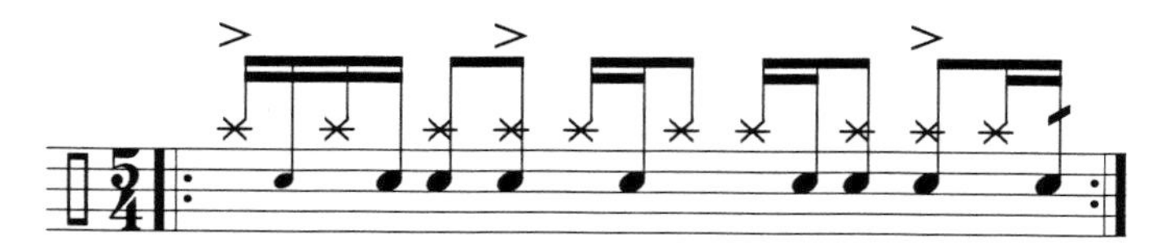

The not-too straight or predictable answer was to create a part in $\frac{5}{4}$, so the back beat or peaks of the beat come on the "+" of count 2 and on count 5 instead of both occurring on downbeats. Here's an example of just the skeleton (or signposts) of the beat.

Example 29F: Skeleton

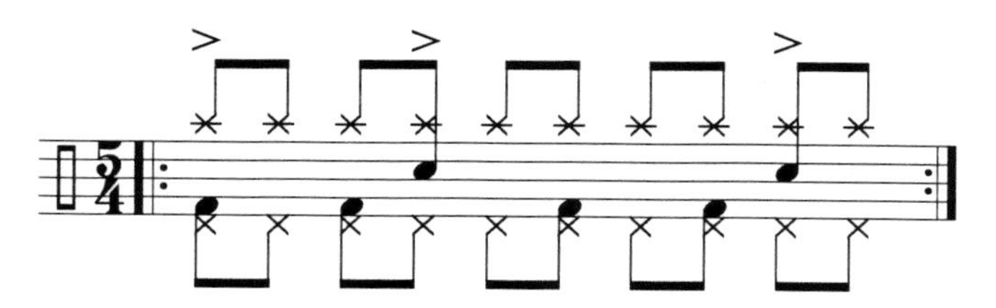

WEEK 30

CRICKET CONQUERS CAVE

On Fillmore from *On Fillmore*

This beat, taken from the first studio record of my long-time duo with St. Louis bassist Darin Gray, was written to accompany the bass line that Darin came up with for this section of the piece. Darin writes these beautiful and complex lines without ever considering what time signature they might be in. I guess it really doesn't matter at all, as the feel, groove, and shape of the lines are what ultimately give them personality, not how they can be broken down mathematically. This slippery little line happens to be in $\frac{7}{4}$. I've included the sticking to show how the right hand basically stays parked on the cowbell, and the left hand moves between the floor tom and snare drum (with the snares turned off). All the drag figures are also executed as open double strokes.

Example 30A: Cricket Conquers Cave

A bar of $\frac{7}{4}$ is basically just alternating bars of $\frac{4}{4}$ and $\frac{3}{4}$, as written here.

Example 30B

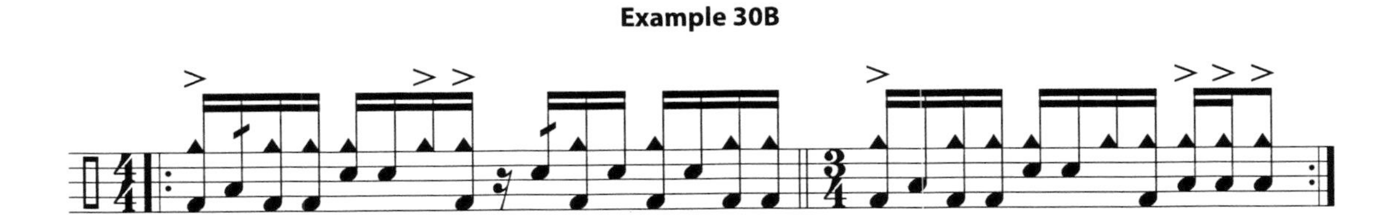

Back in 7 again, let's break it down to just the hands and on one surface to better internalize what's happening with this beat. I'm writing the double stops here as flams, but they should be played as double stops or flat flams.

Example 30C: Hands Only on One Surface

Now let's do the same thing on two surfaces, playing the snare notes on the snare, and the floor tom and cowbell notes on the floor tom. So, only the left hand is moving between two surfaces while the right hand remains on the floor tom.

Example 30D

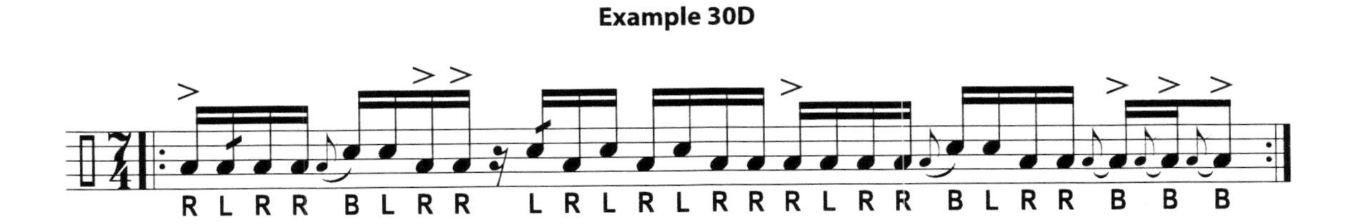

Try adding one more surface by moving the right hand to the cowbell.

Example 30E: Right Hand on Cowbell

Now try adding the left foot. I keep the hi-hat pretty heavily prepared with lots of antique Korean shaman bells, jingle rings, or hi-hat shakers attached via clutches to the hi-hat rod. This helps to keep the time, of course, but it also flavors the beat with more percussive color. Additionally, with all of the attachments on the hi-hat, it helps make that part more audible since the rest of the drums and bass are playing strong. Depending on what kind of a mood I'm in for any particular performance, I'll put the hi-hat (left foot) part on either the downbeats or the upbeats. And, as you'll see, the effect on the beat is substantial. I like it both ways, but the entire groove character of the beat is changed depending on which hi-hat pattern is being played.

Example 30F: Hi-Hat on Downbeats

Example 30G: Hi-Hat on Upbeats

As with any of these beats, I encourage you to experiment after learning them. Try different voicings, putting the doubles in different spots, or even editing out certain counts and morphing it into a different time signature. Also, try voicing the right-hand cowbell part on 3 or 5 temple blocks, or on a mallet percussion instrument. The addition of pitches and a melodic line to the one-limb part can completely alter the beat. Make it your own!

ACCIDENTAL CHASE

On Fillmore from *On Fillmore*

As in the previous beat from "Cricket Conquers Cave," "Accidental Chase" is another odd-time beat constructed to match one of Darin Gray's sinewy upright bass lines. On Fillmore is fond of exploring the slight and super subtle evolutions or degradations from playing a static, locked groove over and over. These explorations give the beat a life of its own. Since these grooves tend to be challenging, the possibility for alterations is heightened due to physical and mental exhaustion. So when you're learning these On Fillmore beats and would like to get the full effect, repeat them without pause for 3, 5, or 10 minutes. This will allow you to experience them as we do!

The drum part for this beat has its origins in an experience I had in college at the University of Kentucky studying under James B. Campbell. One semester, Jim went on sabbatical and studied different kinds of hand drumming. When he came back, he had a whole array of African, Indian, and Middle Eastern drums. Jim would frequently bring in different clinicians and, when he brought in people like John Bergamo or Phil Faini, it exposed me to non-Western ways of thinking about rhythm, drumming, and technique. This of course had a huge impact on my musical development. One of the concepts that stuck with me was the use of open and closed tones in many of these traditions. Whether on Indian tabla, Middle Eastern tar and dumbek, or African djembe or skin drums, open strokes and dead strokes seemed to be ubiquitous. There are examples of Western drumming that also incorporate these techniques, such as the stick shot (think of the solos of Buddy Rich, Max Roach, or Gene Krupa). Or, think about how many rock drummers bury the bass drum beater into the bass drum head or slam down a rimshot back beat on the snare drum with little or no resultant rebound. Even brush technique can be a good example of playing into or out of the head to extract wildly disparate sounds.

After Jim returned from his sabbatical, one particular piece we learned on a set of African drums was the direct inspiration for the "Accidental Chase" groove. The part I had in the African drumming ensemble required me to play two open strokes, followed by two dead strokes. This meant I had to bury the sticks into the skin, which not only achieved a sound with little resonance but also caused a slight pitch bend. Let's start with taking that basic idea in a $\frac{4}{4}$ context.

Example 31A: Accidental Chase

Now, try the same thing but accenting the open strokes. In order to get enough contrast between the open and closed strokes, I make sure there's a big difference in height between the two.

Example 31B: With Open Stroke Accent

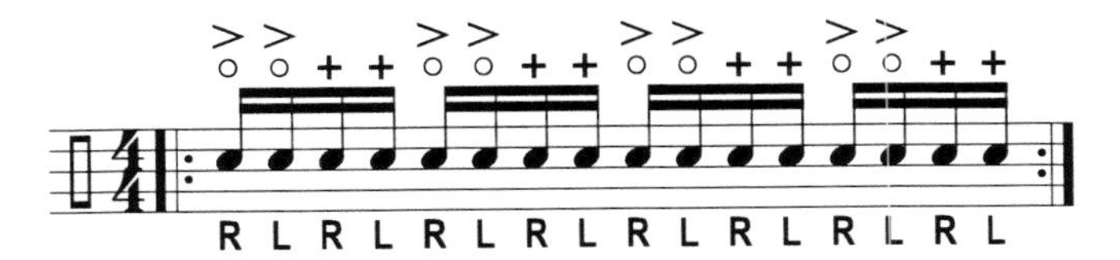

Since I alternate the order of the accents in the beat, try the exact same thing with the accents displaced by two subdivisions.

Example 31C: Upbeat Open Stroke Accent

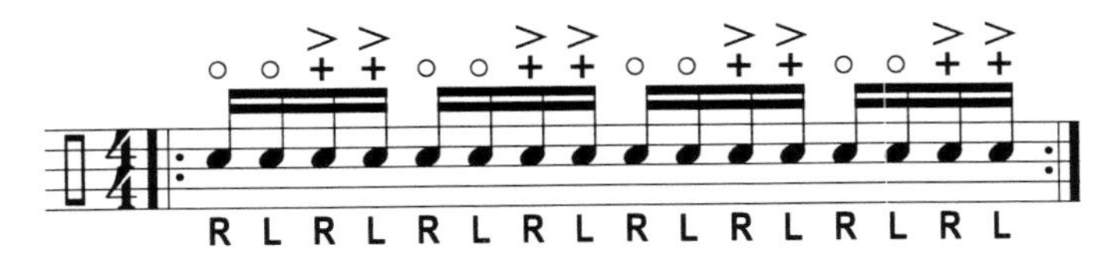

Let's try a stripped down version of the beat in the proper time signature of $\frac{11}{8}$. This example has the stickings added. Note how this beat is just the same rhythmic material twice in a row. That is, two groups of four followed by a group of three (repeated). The group of three is indicated by the right hand moving over to the floor tom.

Example 31D: Hands Only Skeleton

The bass drum simply marks the beginning of the cells of four- and three-note groupings.

Example 31E: With Bass Drum

Now, let's add the open and closed tones. Start slow in order for your muscles to get used to playing the dead strokes.

Example 31F: With Bass Drum and Open/Closed Strokes

Next, let's take a stab at adding the accent pattern into the beat. Remember, the sequence of open and closed tones stays the same for both halves of the beat, but the placement of accents changes. Be sure to exaggerate the difference between the accented and unaccented notes, and remember to keep the snares off for this beat. I keep the heads relatively loose when I know I'll be playing this song. This causes the dead strokes to produce a better sounding sonic personality. It also adds that little bit of pitch bend I mentioned earlier. Here's the final beat as I play it live and on the record.

Example 31G: Full Beat

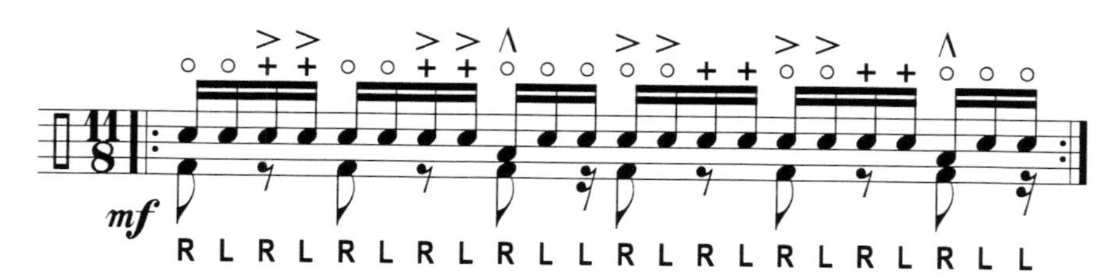

APOSTOLIC

Loose Fur from *Born Again in the USA*

This song, from the second Loose Fur record, goes through several shifts in both meter and feel. With this band, a lot of the parts are written while jamming in the studio. That's why some of the meters seem like different people might be playing in different times. This song has a section that embodies this with all three of us playing in different time signatures, but all starting and stopping together. The beat I'm going to focus on here though is the opposite. For this two-bar beat in $\frac{5}{4}$, there is a clear-cut association between the guitar part and the drums.

Let's look at the first measure. The right hand keeps things locked down by laying down solid quarter notes on the cowbell. The bass and snare drums play with the guitar until the end of the measure, at which time the bass drum switches to an off-beat figure on count 4 instead of staying on the beat with the guitar.

Example 32A: Apostolic (0:32)
First Measure

♩ = 152

f

The second measure does what the first does not: it stays with the guitar part and cadences on the downbeats with it.

Example 32B: Second Measure

When you put them together, you get this:

Example 32C: Full Beat

CHAPTER 9

Beats with Melody

WEEK 33

WILD THINGS

Glenn Kotche, unreleased

In this chapter, we're going to examine beats in which one voice, or limb, splits up a given line amongst several surfaces to create melody. This is especially true when the melody of the beat is played on pitched percussion instruments such as crotales, kalimba, almglocken, or orchestra bells. The first beat presented does more than that; three limbs break up lines with only the hi-hat (left foot) keeping things grounded. This is a solo piece I play live, but have yet to record (although there are videos out there of the song). The right half of the body covers the main groove, which is split between the bass drum, rack tom, floor tom, and five-pitched almglocken or tuned alpine cowbells. I think it only makes sense to learn this one additively, putting the pieces together one by one and making sure the foundation of the beat is solid and comfortable.

The key to this is really just getting the kinesthetic, or muscle, memory down. Since you most likely won't be able to look at everything you're playing while playing it, sometimes you may have to let one of your arms go on trust alone! Once you familiarize yourself with the movements and choreography of the individual components of the beat, it's just a matter of putting them all together and getting to a place of flow. In the interest of keeping things concise, I'll just give a brief description of what's happening with each new and developing incarnation of the beat as it evolves into the final example. Keep in mind that the crotale melody here, as is the case with the almglocken melody, can be played on any pitched instrument. Also, this beat is just one of the melodic lines that occurs in the piece. I chose this as a good representative of the overall nature of the piece because this melody is the most fun to play in my opinion as well.

We begin with the right-hand bell part, which is simplified to be played on one bell instead of five.

Example 33A: Wild Things
Bell Pattern on One Bell

Next, add the quarter-note hi-hat part.

Example 33B: With Hi-Hat

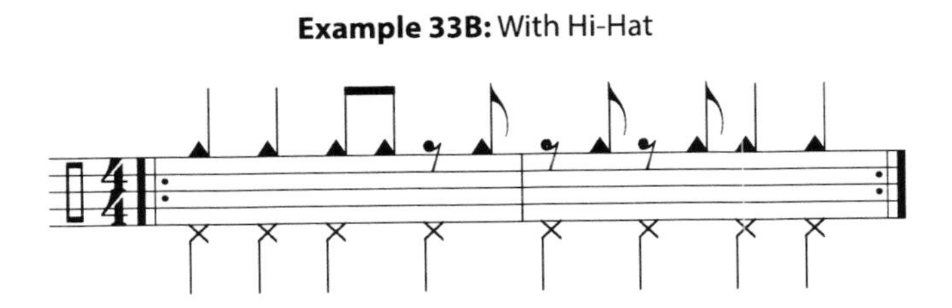

Now leave the hi-hat out and just try the simplified bell and bass drum part together.

Example 33C: Bell and Bass Drum

Now, add the hi-hat back in so we have both feet and the simplified bell pattern. This can get a little tricky since the feet go back and forth from playing in unison to playing opposite of one another.

Example 33D: Bell, Hi-Hat, and Bass Drum

Next, let's try the simplified bell pattern with the rack and floor tom parts added in.

Example 33E: Right-Hand Part Orchestrated

Leaving the tom part out this time, just try the bell part (which is no longer simplified) but split it amongst the five pitches.

Example 33F: Bell Part Orchestrated

Next, add the tom parts back in again.

Example 33G: Right-Hand Part on Bells and Toms

Now, add the bass drum part in with these.

Example 33H: Right-Hand Part on Bells and Toms with Bass Drum

And finally, add the hi-hat pulse and we have all of the non-crotale elements of the beat in place.

Example 33I: Full Drum Part

Next, while keeping the hi-hat quarter-note pulse, learn the melody part with the left hand. There are only two notes that are different between the first half and the second half of the melody. The rhythm is the same, so don't get discouraged by it being eight bars long!

Example 33J: Left-Hand Melodic Line with Hi-Hat

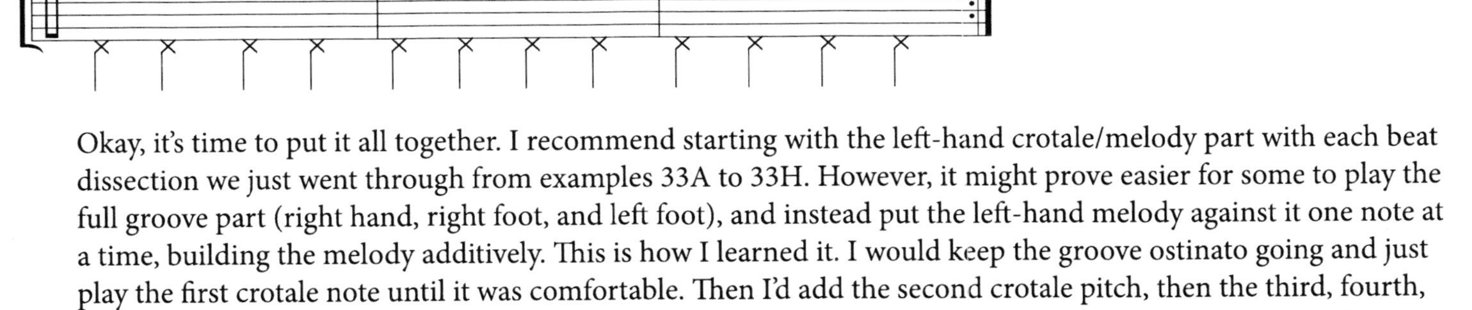

Okay, it's time to put it all together. I recommend starting with the left-hand crotale/melody part with each beat dissection we just went through from examples 33A to 33H. However, it might prove easier for some to play the full groove part (right hand, right foot, and left foot), and instead put the left-hand melody against it one note at a time, building the melody additively. This is how I learned it. I would keep the groove ostinato going and just play the first crotale note until it was comfortable. Then I'd add the second crotale pitch, then the third, fourth, fifth, etc. until I was playing the entire melody with the groove part (the full beat). Try both ways, and whichever method works best for you can serve as an example of how to approach future beats of this complexity level.

Example 33K: Full Beat

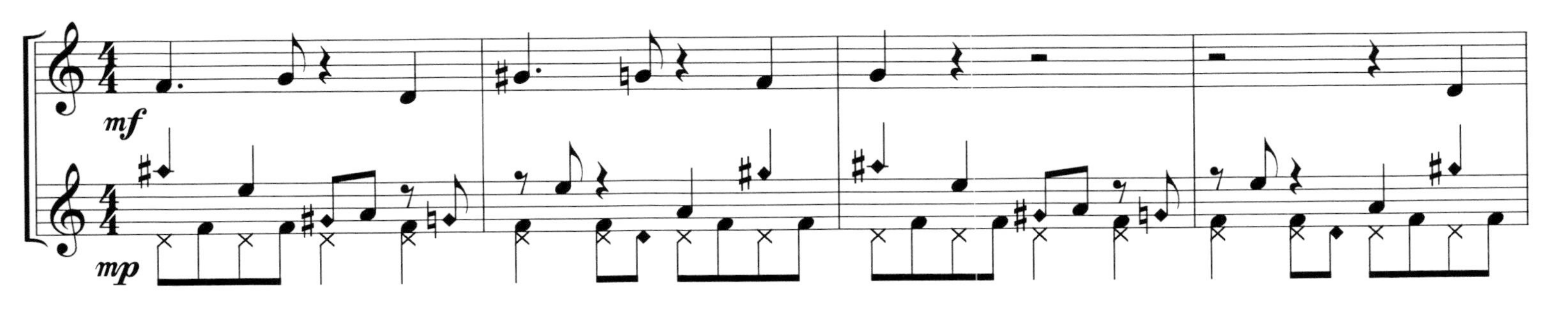

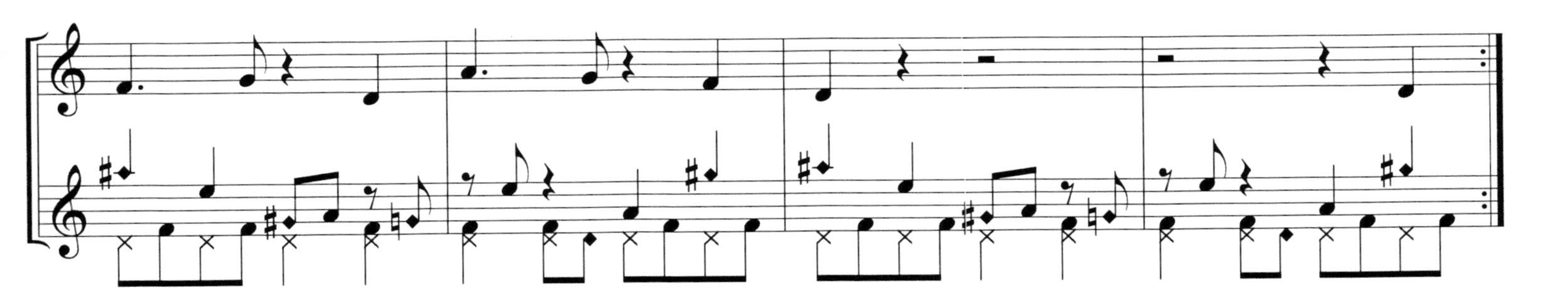

RADIO CURE

Wilco from *Yankee Hotel Foxtrot*

After "Wild Things," this beat will be a breeze! The main groove is a pulse with little inflections, and fills thrown in at random. I first keep the pulse on the floor toms, and use soft felt mallets to occasionally play quiet color splashes by gently striking the cymbals with sizzlers attached to them. When I play the song live, I reinforce the pulse with bass-drum quarter notes and hi-hat splashes on 2 and 4.

For the second verse, I switch from mallets to maracas in order to sustain the floor-tom pulse. For the chorus, I keep the pulse going with my right hand while the left hand plays a melodic line on crotales or vibes under the vocals. Here is an example of the pulse part.

Example 34A: Radio Cure
Drum Part

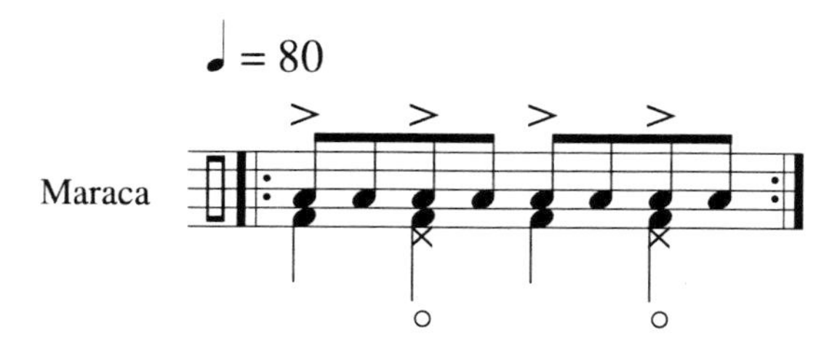

And, here is the melody part. It's one measure repeated four times and resolves with the first note sustaining and decaying naturally.

Example 34B: Melody (Left Hand)

Now, simply put them together.

Example 34C: Full Beat (2:27)

I AM TRYING TO BREAK YOUR HEART

Wilco from *Yankee Hotel Foxtrot*

This is the first song off the first Wilco record I recorded. The body of the song consists of five verses before the only chorus comes in. Since the verses basically consist of three strummed chords repeated over and over under the lyric, it's up to the other instruments to help the song evolve. The drums are one element that help provide scene changes as the song unfolds, helping reframe the static progression and the lyric with each new verse.

A steady, standard back beat groove would do the opposite of what the song needed, so I had to come up with some other options. When I was playing and bouncing ideas off the other guys in the band, a couple of options rose to the top. Both of these were a little off-kilter. Because I couldn't decide which one I liked best, our singer (Jeff Tweedy) suggested I just play both. So I did, usually alternating between the two. The disjunct nature of the beat fit perfectly into the architecture of the song as it was mixed and arranged by Jim O'Rourke. It starts with sonic chaos and slowly comes into focus over the five verses with the drum groove eventually straightening out into a more traditional rock beat. When the one and only chorus arrives, the drums drop out, which helps direct the listener to the chorus lyric. The song then devolves back into chaos.

In addition to the drum parts, I also added several layers of percussion including vibraphone, shaker, piano string scrapes, ceramic floor tiles, hubcap, super ball mallets and drink mixers on piano strings and crotales. When it came to learning the song for our live show, I was faced with the dilemma of figuring out which parts to play and which to leave out. I came up with a composite part that I think covers all of the main elements. That's what we'll learn here. Let's start with the first half of the beat. Both versions of the beat begin with the same first measure.

Example 35A: I Am Trying to Break Your Heart (1:27)
First Half

The hubcap instrument is just that, a hubcap from a car. For this recording, I bought a great sounding one at an actual hubcap store. I set it on a snare drum stand, affixed a contact mic to it, and ran that through an amplifier. The hubcap was also close mic'd. It just provided an unusual and intriguing sound in the beat that wasn't a cymbal or tom-tom. Next, let's add the second half of the first beat.

Example 35B: With the Second Half of the First Beat

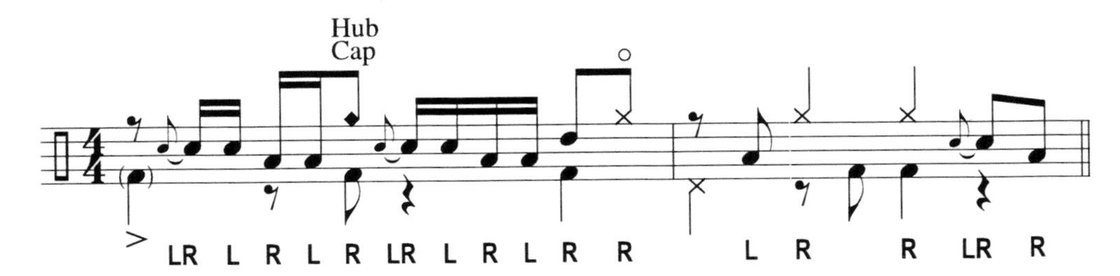

Now, add the second half of the second beat.

Example 35C: With the Second Half of the Second Beat

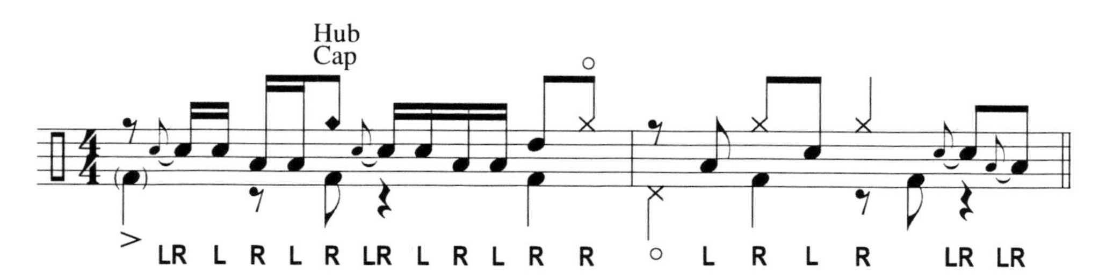

There's a few times in the song where I add a little crotale line at the end of the second beat. It looks like this:

Example 35D: With Melodic Part

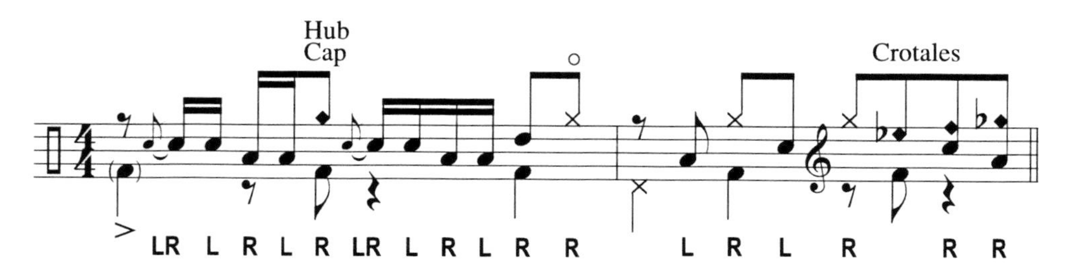

So, the whole phrase looks like this:

Example 35E: Full Beat

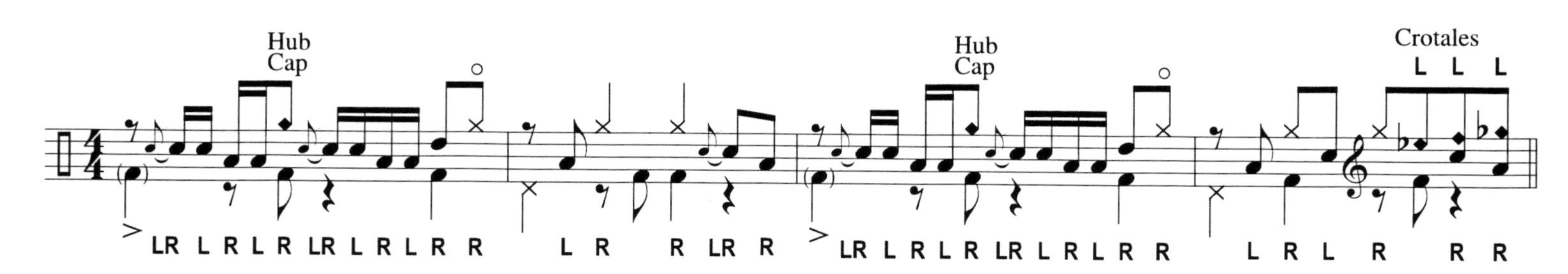

KAMERA

Wilco from *Yankee Hotel Foxtrot*

This is a song I tend to use as an example in lessons of how a drum part can develop and evolve over the course of a song. The beats I play live for "Kamera" grew out of necessity—I needed to make composite parts (similar to other beats in this book) of multiple drum passes, percussion, and vibraphone parts. Covering all the beats in this song is a lot of material to go through, and since this chapter addresses beats that have pitched content, we'll skip right to the very last beat in the song. For this beat, I just needed to combine a straightforward drum part and a vibraphone line (which I play on crotales when I do this beat live). Let's begin with the drum parts. Remember, this is only using your right hand and bass drum.

Example 36A: Kamera (2:41)
Hi-Hat, Snare Drum, and Bass Drum

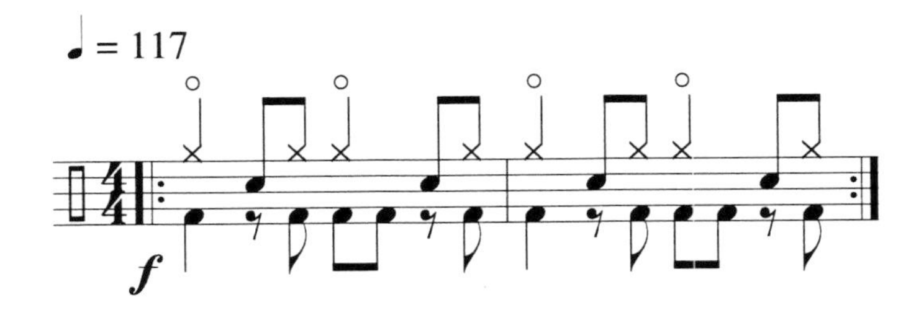

Now, let's try the melody independent of everything else. This will be played with your left hand only.

Example 36B: Melody

Before we throw the two together, let's try a skeleton version of the melody first. This beat is difficult, not just because one hand is playing drums and the other a pitched instrument, but also because the shape of the melodic part is in three-note groupings. Therefore, your left hand is cycling through a motion every three notes while your right hand is cycling every two or four notes depending on how you look at it. Let's just take the first note of each melodic grouping and put that against what the right hand is doing.

Example 36C: Simplified Drums with Melody Skeleton

Next, try the same thing with the left hand melody part (just the core notes), but this time play that against the full drum beat.

Example 36D: Full Drums with Melody Skeleton

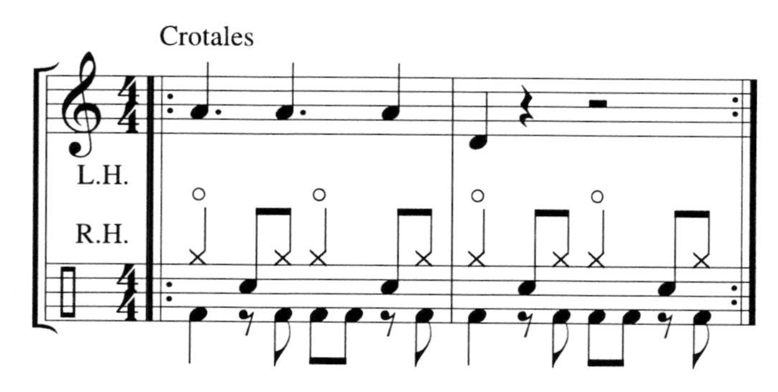

And finally, put it all together. As I've stated elsewhere, take it *slow* at first. I'd also suggest trying just one of the melodic three-note groupings first. Then try the first and second groupings (six pitches total), and work your way up to the entire phrase.

Example 36E: Full Beat

CHAPTER 10

Tom-Centric Beats

LIFE LEFT HIM THERE

The Minus 5 from *Down With Wilco*

This beat is taken from the chorus of the song and is basically comprised of a run going from the snare drum down the toms of a standard four-piece drumset. It's a very easily executed beat, but effective. It does have a slightly march-like quality due to the snare drum part and quarter-note pulse on the bass drum. But the toms help break up that association and give a rolling downward phrase that keeps the momentum up. Here is the beat.

Example 37A: Life Left Him There (1:12)

This beat was inspired by a band I was listening to a lot around the time I recorded this song in September 2001. The band was Joy Division and the record I couldn't get enough of was *Closer*. On the opening track of that record, "Atrocity Exhibition," Stephen Morris plays a measured run down the toms that's the perfect part for the song. The drum part sets up a metronomic groove, cold and calculated but still grooving, and it's perfect. He does a slight augmentation by adding in the snare drum at points, but the main beat goes something like this and as you can see, I owe a debt of gratitude to Mr. Morris for coming up with such a great part.

Example 37B: Atrocity Exhibition

WEEK 38

ANOTHER NIGHT ON THIS EARTH

Paul K & The Weathermen from *Love Is a Gas*

This is the last Paul K. & The Weathermen record I played on at the close of my tenure with the band. This record was produced by one of my drumming heroes, Maureen Tucker, who was the primary drummer in The Velvet Underground, one of the most influential bands of all time.

Maureen was definitely a hands-on producer when it came to her area of expertise, the drums. This is something I welcomed with open arms since I loved her economy and part composition on those first several Velvet Underground records. When we recorded this record, some of the songs she left alone when it came to the drum parts, but this one she was hands on, directing me on parts and the actual architecture of the beat. She built this beat up, one voice at a time. Basically, I was the puppet and she was the puppet master!

This beat perfectly demonstrates Maureen's sensibility when it comes to constructing the perfect part for a song. That's why her parts are so memorable. Whether it's the ultra-economical tambourine back beat on "Pale Blue Eyes" or the driving toms on "Sister Ray" or "Heroin," she seemed to always come up with the right part for the song—and never with any flash or flare. It was all stripped down to the most essential rhythms to carry the song whether that was supportive or conversely tribal and brutal. She played some great parts featuring toms and tambourine on songs like "Venus in Furs" or "All Tomorrow's Parties." These parts are of the same ilk as the part she had me play on this song.

Let's start with the basic beat, which is played on two toms with the bass drum reinforcing the floor tom.

Example 38A: Another Night on This Earth (0:10)

Next, she had me overdub a tambourine back beat. Now even though these next two parts were overdubs, I eventually had to figure out how to play them live. So basically I ended up playing the tambourine part with my left foot on the hi-hat with a couple of jingle ring attachments.

Example 38B: With Hi-Hat Tambourine

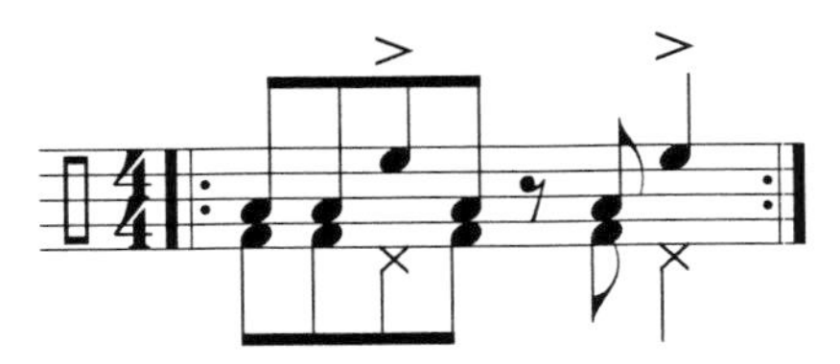

Then came the quarter-note pulse on a large cowbell. Live, I played this with my right hand (with the cowbell off to my right) and had my left hand cover the tom parts using a felt timpani mallet.

Example 38C: With Cowbell

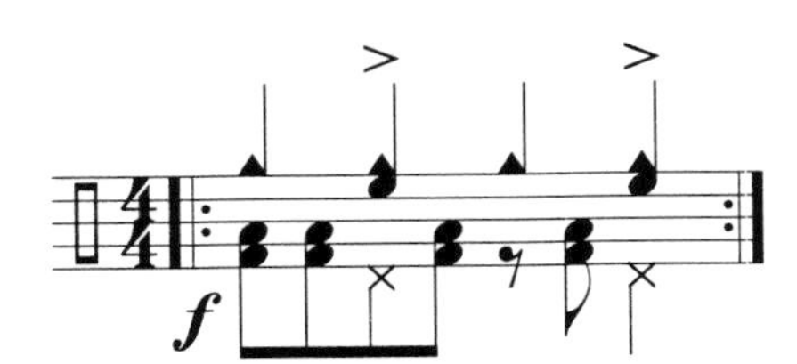

As you can see, the left hand matches up with the bass drum when playing the floor tom, and it matches up with the hi-hat (tambo) when playing the rack tom. It makes this beat a good basic independence exercise in the rock idiom by splitting up the left hand allegiance between both feet, while the right hand holds things down with a quarter-note pulse or ride pattern.

WISHFUL THINKING

Wilco from *A Ghost Is Born*

The origins of this groove came from a couple of sources.

When I was playing in Paul K. & The Weathermen, we played a song called "The Grid." Since this song was recorded before I was in the band, I stayed true to the drum parts by my predecessor, Tim Welch—parts I loved and thought were perfect for the song. Although I would play around with the specifics from night to night, I always played it open handed, riding on the hi-hat with my left hand, which allowed my right hand to easily play the tom notes. Tim's main beat went something like this:

Example 39A: The Grid

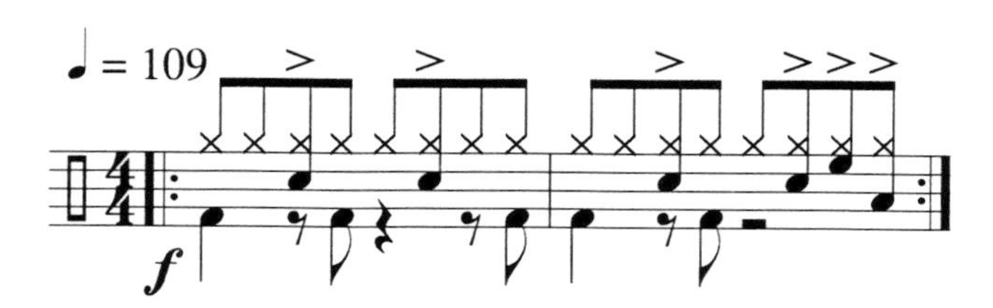

When I asked Tim about the beat, he said he was inspired by a Ringo Starr beat that was somewhat similar to what he'd come up with for the song. I can't remember exactly which Beatles song it was, but both "In My Life" and "All I've Got to Do" have a similar type of accent pattern. Those brilliantly sparse beats go like this:

Example 39B: In My Life

Example 39C: All I've Got to Do

I think all of these beats might have been in the back of my mind when I heard the guitar strumming rhythm in the section of "Wishful Thinking" we're addressing here. What came out was a variation or hybrid of those beats. This example is a slight variation from the original that appears on *A Ghost Is Born* as well. All of these beats share the same type of clave in that at least one of the back beats or accents of each beat is displaced to an upbeat instead of landing on beats 2 and 4. The one crucial difference here is that I draped cloth napkins over the heads of the snare drum and toms, much like Ringo was known to do on many songs. When we perform this song live, I even prepare the drums with those (with Nathaniel Murphy's preparation and help). Also, I'm using general timpani mallets with medium-hard felt mallet heads. Like those other beats that I cited, this beat is also a two-measure phrase, and I play it open-handed just like I used to do with "The Grid."

Example 39D: Wishful Thinking (1:12)

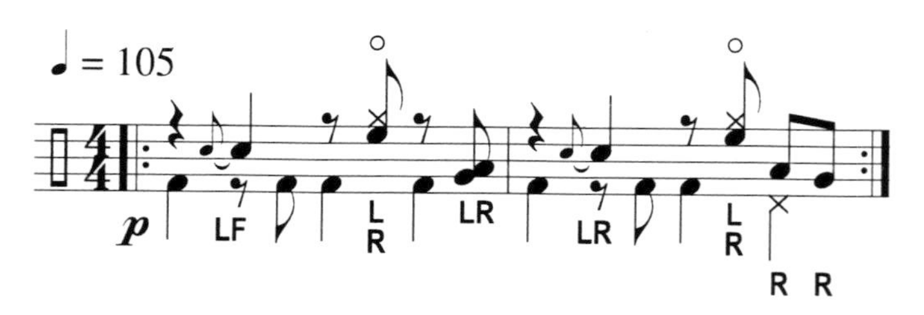

WEEK 40

ELEGANT TRANSACTION

Loose Fur from *Loose Fur*

This beat is from the final section of the song, which is basically a coda. This beat is similar to the one I play in my solo version of the "Balinese Monkey Chant" which appears on my record *Mobile,* as well as the *2006 Modern Drummer Festival DVD.* The main pulse is alternating sixteenth notes between the floor tom and the bass drum. This creates a kind of tribal drone for the rest of the music to ride on top of. There's a kind of double-time back beat added on top of that base played on snare drum and a deep rack tom. The floor tom and hi-hat play in unison throughout the beat. It looks like this:

Example 40A: Elegant Transaction (2:33)
Floor Tom and Hi-Hat

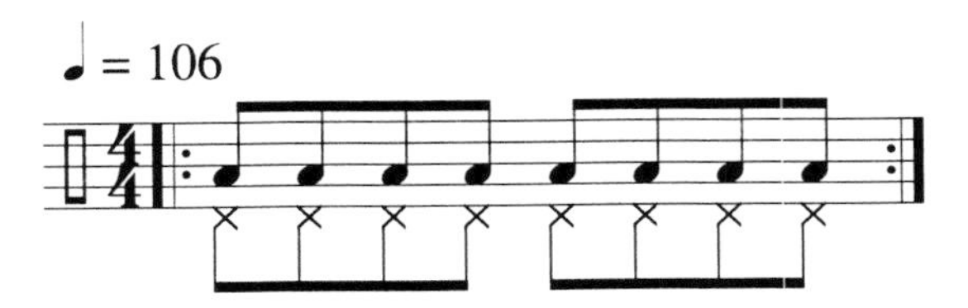

It is offset and complemented by the upbeat sixteenth notes on the bass drum. I find it easiest to learn this part by building it piece by piece starting with one count, then two, three and finally the full measure.

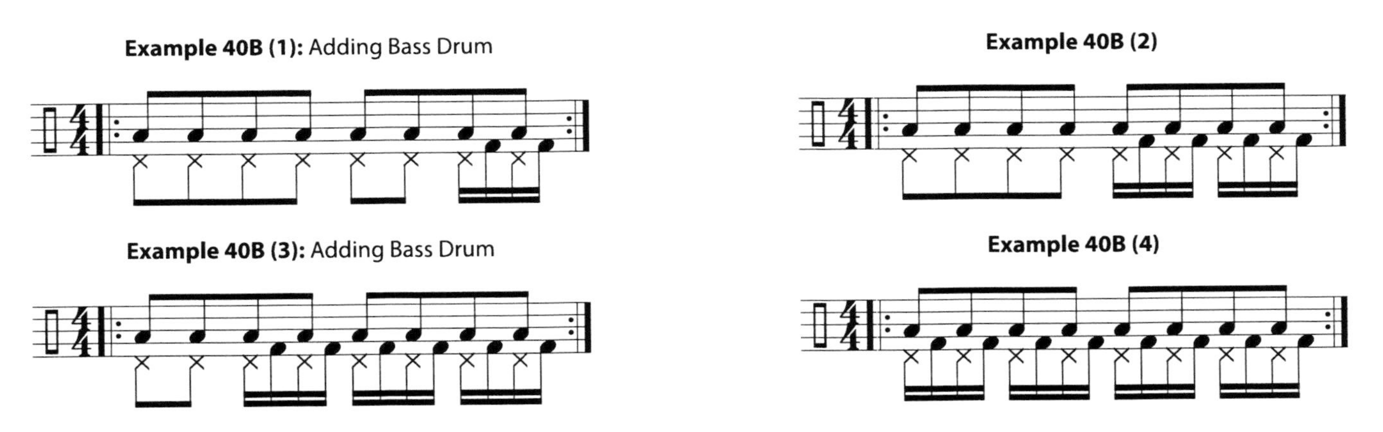

Next, let's try the snare and tom hits with just the floor tom and hi-hat eighth notes underneath.

Example 40C: Adding the Left-Hand Voices

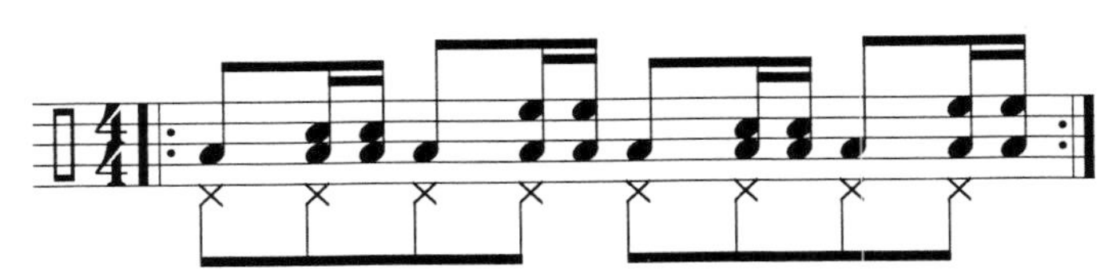

And finally, let's put it all together. This beat is ripe for experimentation and I suggest you play around with where the back beat falls both rhythmically, as well as how to voice it.

Example 40D: Full Beat

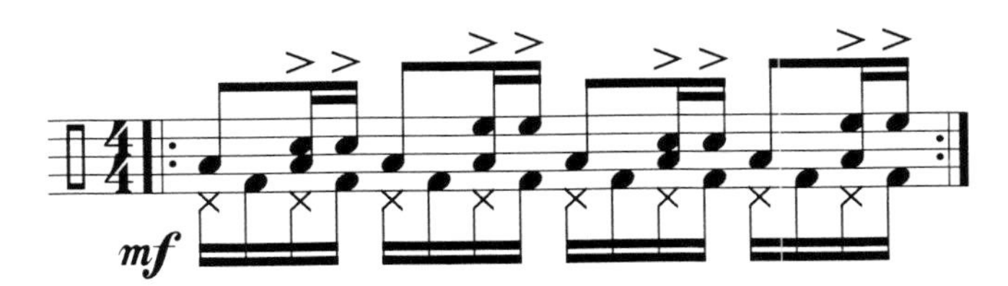

CHAPTER 11

Beats Inspired by Other Beats

WEEK 41

PLEASE PATRONIZE OUR SPONSORS

Jim O'Rourke from *Eureka*

I mentioned the bossa nova back in week 22 regarding the bass drum and hi-hat pattern. This beat is from the very first Jim O'Rourke record I played on. I guess it was soon enough after I finished college that all of my "essential styles" of standard drumset beats were still fresh in my memory and I drew upon or customized the bossa nova into what I'll call a bossa-rock variation. First, let's start by dissecting the individual elements of the bossa nova beginning with the bass drum heartbeat (or ostinato).

Example 41A: Bossa Nova Bass Drum Pattern

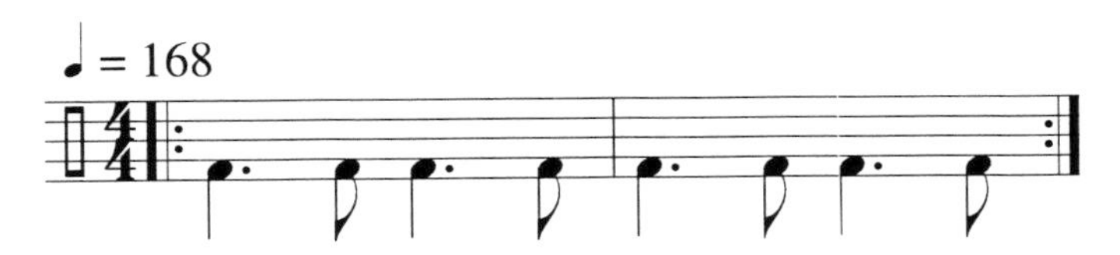

Now, add the hi-hat part played with the left foot. Essentially, this is also a slowed down version of a samba drumset foot pattern. These voices were originally adapted for the drumset from the open and closed sounds of the surdo (or marching bass drum).

Example 41B: Bossa Feet

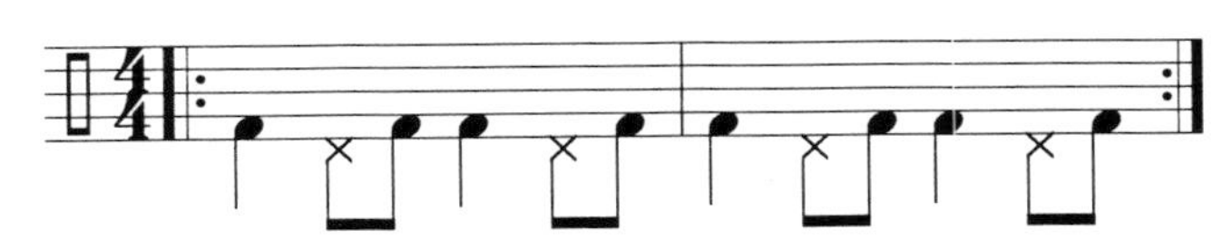

Next, let's try the steady right-hand part. This is typically played on a closed hi-hat and emulates the shaker part in a bossa nova, along with the snare drum left hand cross-stick/clave part. The clave part is the rhythmic melody of the bossa nova and was originally played on, you guessed it—claves.

Example 41C: Bossa Hands

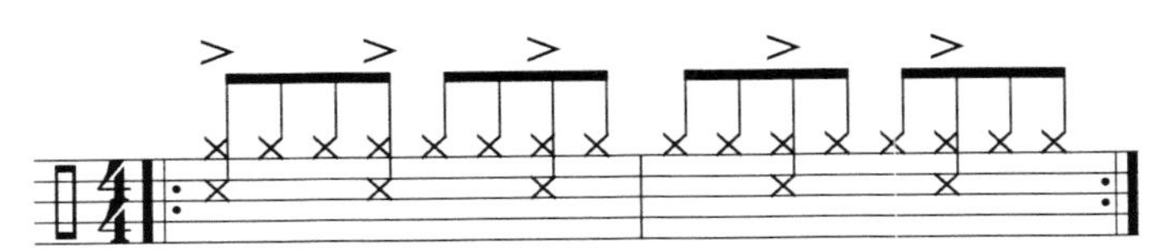

It's a good idea to try the clave part isolated with the feet, as I've found it to be the trickiest part for students to learn. This is because the cross-stick will sometimes line up with the bass drum, sometimes it's just before the bass drum, and sometimes just after. The inconsistency of where it lands against the bass drum tends to throw people off at first.

Example 41D: Bossa Clave and Feet

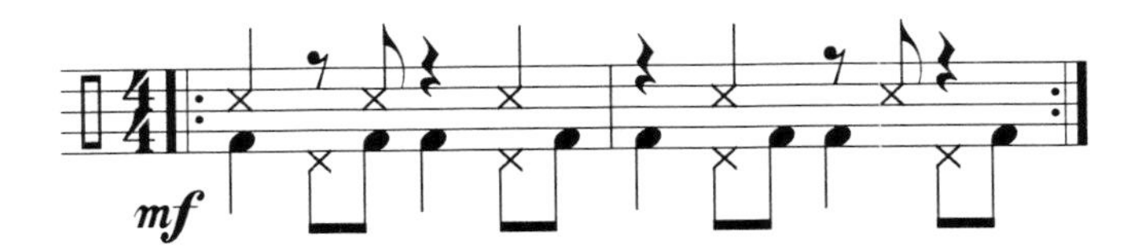

Now, let's try all of the voices in tandem. As I mentioned before, if this proves difficult, do the obvious and play it slowly! You can also try vamping on all of the ostinato parts (bass drum, hi-hat with foot, and hi-hat with right hand), and by adding one cross stick/clave note at a time. So, just loop the repeating parts. When things lock in, add a note—one at a time—until you get the full pattern. It's important to note that this is an example of a basic 3:2 clave pattern. Remember, there are other claves and variations that are handy to know. Don't be too respectful of the original but instead use it as a model that you can draw from to create original beats that suit the song at hand.

Example 41E: Bossa Nova Full Beat

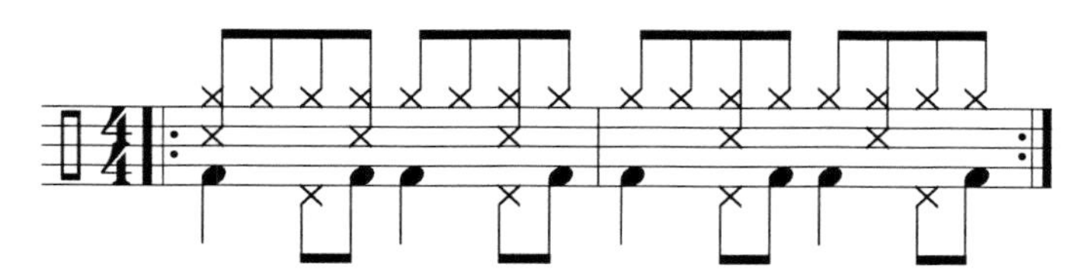

For "Please Patronize Our Sponsors," I keep the bass drum pattern the same as the bossa nova we just covered. I do change the clave part, however, making it a bit more back beat-like in where it lands. And, I also forego the cross stick for a regular snare drum hit. In addition, I add a couple of hi-hat openings to help flavor the beat a bit. Try the foot pattern with the new clave first.

Example 41F: Bass Drum and Snare Drum

Then just try the hi-hat right hand part, the hi-hat left foot part, and the snare drum part. So, all we're leaving off is the bass drum.

Example 41G: Hi-Hat with Foot, Hand, and Snare Drum

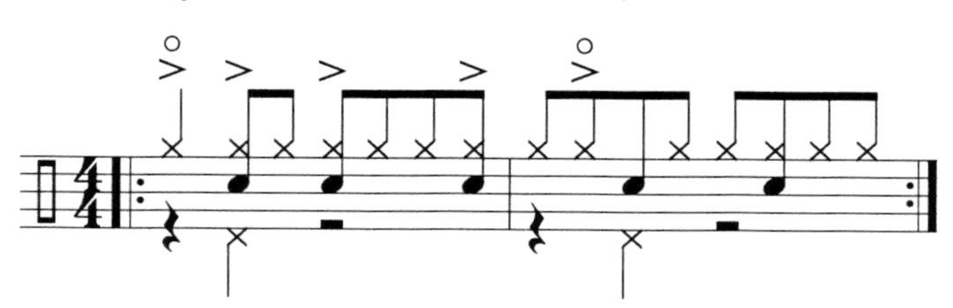

Now, put it all together. Try playing four-bar phrases of a bossa nova, alternating with four-bar phrases of this beat. And, please come up with your own variations and clave patterns.

Example 41H: Full Beat (0:31)

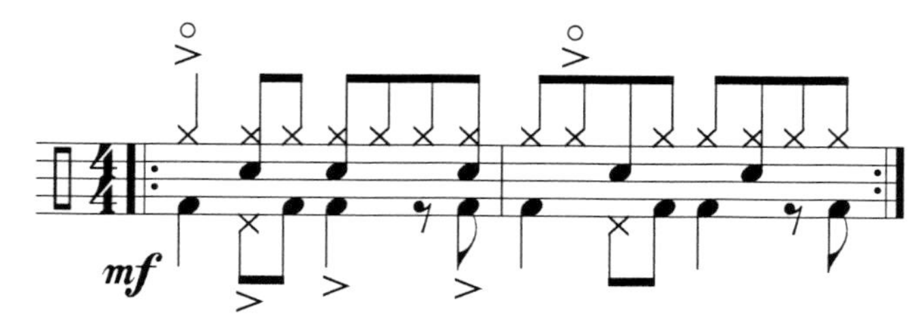

Even though I rarely (if ever) am required to play a bossa nova, samba, soca, rhumba, meringue, calypso, or Mozambique, etc., I am forever grateful I learned all of these types of beats. There are specific skills required to play all of them that you might never come across if you only learn rock beats or only work on jazz independence or swing time. I use the fundamentals and concepts behind these beats as a basis for creating and adapting new beats that might add a certain quality that is just what a song needs—regardless of what style of music it is. Remember, you can use the principles of any of these beats. And, by customizing, you'll lose any baggage they come with. This means a beat based on a soca, for instance, doesn't have to sound like a soca unless you want it to.

BORN ALONE (chorus)

Wilco from *The Whole Love*

Earlier, we took a look at the verse beat from this song (week 8), so now let's check out the beat from the chorus of the song. Unlike the verse beat, which was inspired by an idea I'd been thinking about—moving the time keeping from the ride to other voices, in that case, the bass drum—this beat came about by chance really. On the way to the studio on the day Wilco arranged and tracked "Born Alone," I was listening to the classic rock station on the car radio when the song "I Can See for Miles," by The Who, came on. I had covered this song many times in my high school rock band and was familiar with the snare drum sixteenth-note storm in the choruses.

When it came to jamming on "Born Alone," that was the first idea that popped into my head. As great as the Keith Moon part is, it seemed too bare and not quite exciting enough to just play a stream of sixteenth notes on the snare for "Born Alone." It needed a bit more. Just because it worked for "I Can See for Miles," doesn't mean it would be as effective when transferred over to another song. I thought about riding on the crash cymbal instead during the choruses for an explosive sound, and then going back and overdubbing the snare drum machine gun fire Keith Moon part.

Rather than having to overdub, I thought about trying those parts simultaneously. I knew I could approximate something along the lines of some of the patterns I played when I learned Steve Reich's landmark duet for hand clappers, "Clapping Music," as a solo piece (or duet between right and left hand). Since the song was too fast to play constant sixteenth notes with my left hand at the volume that I needed to while riding on the crash cymbal with my right hand, I just left one note of the four note sixteenth grouping out. The pattern "1-e-_-a"—which is just leaving the third of the four notes out—felt much better than the other three options and was very similar to some of those "Clapping Music" patterns when played against the eighth note right-hand pattern. Most importantly, I could pull it off. It's definitely a challenge for me from night to night because of the tempo and the very loud volume I'm required to produce. Luckily, another happy accident makes that part substantially easier for me to execute.

On the first downbeat of the second verse of the song, instead of a loud crash, there's a little cutting bell tone on the record. I actually think our multi-instrumentalist and *The Whole Love* co-producer, Pat Sansone, played it on the record. I love that little twist and knew I wanted to do it live. So, I play it on a crotale. The only problem is that, live, hitting a crotale with a wooden drumstick on a heavily amplified stage yields no sonic results for the audience. I needed to play it with a hard keyboard percussion mallet. Luckily, Pro-Mark made me several different prototypes of drumset mallets that are basically timpani shafts with keyboard mallet heads attached. I have one set with grey polyball heads I already use on the song "I Am Trying to Break Your Heart." I just ended up using that in my left hand along with a normal stick in my right hand for "Born Alone" so I could effectively play that one crotale hit. The happy accident was revealed when I realized that something about the way the drumset mallet was weighted and balanced made it much easier to play the snare drum sixteenth note pattern in the choruses. It might even be due to the large round mallet head eliciting more rebound from the drumhead than a typical stick. It's still a challenge every night, which is good in my opinion, but I know I can pull it off pretty effortlessly by using that mallet.

Let's check out the left-hand part alone to begin with.

Example 42A: Born Alone (Chorus)
Left Hand

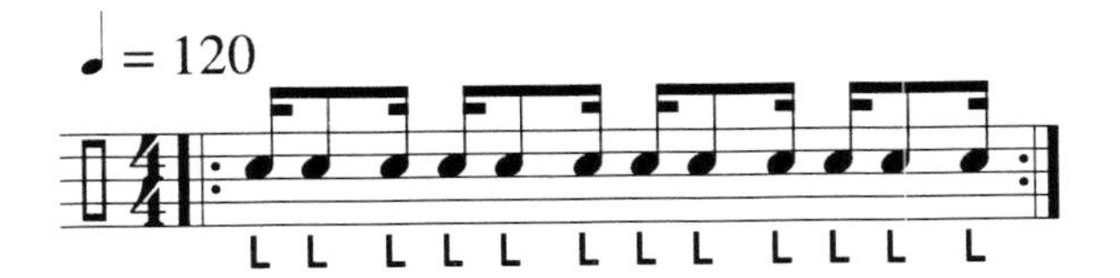

Now, add the feet, and then the right hand.

Example 42B: Snare Drum, Bass Drum, and Hi-Hat

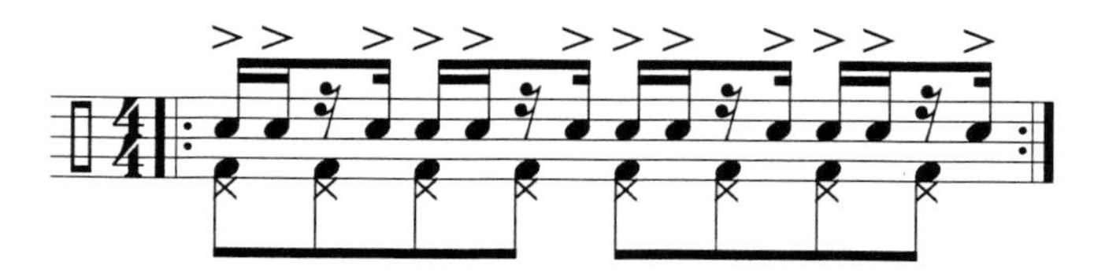

Example 42C: Cymbal and Snare Drum

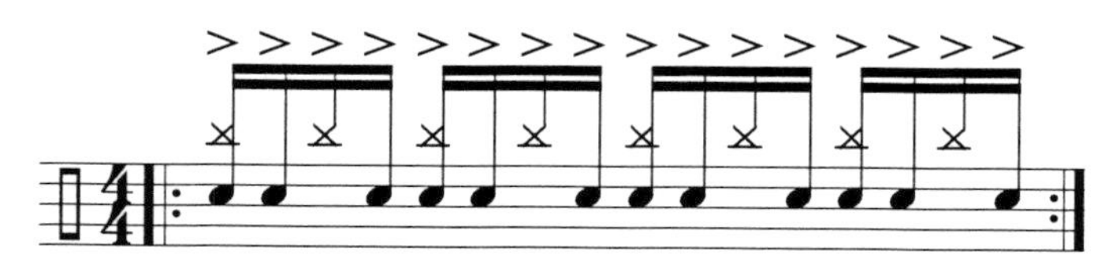

And, with all four limbs together, it looks like this.

Example 42D: Full Beat (1:40)

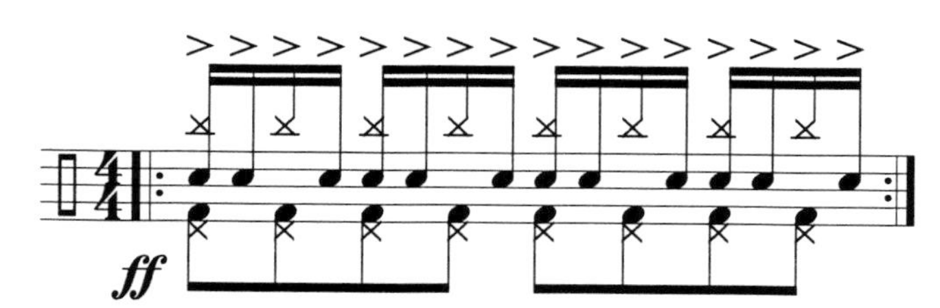

WEEK 43

RISING RED LUNG

Wilco from *The Whole Love*

This beat, from the ending tag portion of the song, actually came about after tracking was completed. Pat Sansone was working on the mix and called me to stop by the studio to add one more part. He didn't know what, but thought there should be a drum part in the little ending coda section before the song fades out. I sat down to play him some ideas and he immediately loved the first one I threw out. Inspired by the rhythm of Nels Cline's electric guitar line at that point, I played something on snare drum that played off of Nels's accents. It was basically some kind of hybrid beat that took elements of New Orleans second-line drumming and a calypso groove. I added a hit on the half open hi-hat on beat 4 as an approximationof a back beat. It sounded vaguely Steve Gadd-like since the snare rolls are similar to his beat on Paul Simon's "50 Ways to Leave Your Lover." But, it was something kind of in between all of these. Let's first examine a basic New Orleans second-line beat. Originally these beats were played by two drummers on marching drums who were in the second line of a funeral procession. The clave, or predominant rhythm here, is the same 3:2 pattern as that of the bossa nova covered in week 41. First, let's just try playing that clave rhythm on the bass drum.

Example 43A: Second-Line Beat Clave

Next, add the snare part, which will just be playing straight eighths (albeit swung and sloppy, with loads of feel). We can also add a hi-hat back beat as well, played with the left foot.

Example 43B: Basic Second-Line Beat

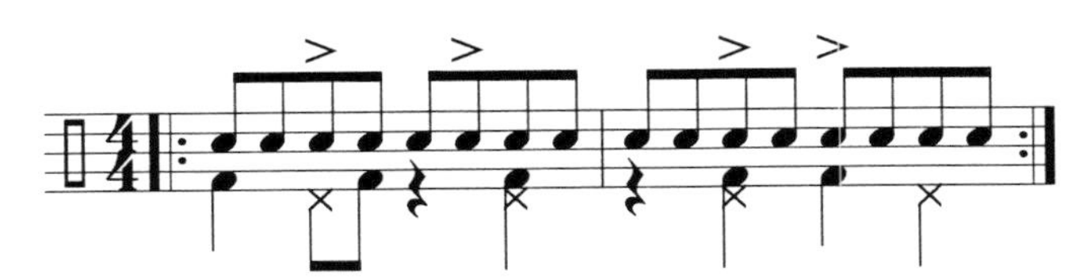

This is the blueprint for a second-line groove. From here, improvise by adding inflections such as accents, buzzes and drags, flams, rim shots, ghost notes, and even omitting notes. One variation I like to play breaks away from the standard bass drum pattern in the second bar. I also like to add a lot of swung-out buzz rolls and flams into the mix as well. Here is the basic beat without any of the flair.

Example 43C: Second-Line Variation

Now, let's look at the same skeleton but written in double time. This doesn't necessarily mean it's faster. It's just another way of writing it out.

Example 43D: Written in Double Time

And finally, let's check out the beat I play at that end part of "Rising Red Lung." The first two bass drum notes give the entire beat its rhythmic character. The accented doubles on the snare are just a way to soften and add flow to that accent. And, the final hi-hat hit covers the last accent in the clave pattern. So, you can see, I play the first two accents on bass drum, the third on snare drum (with doubles), the fourth is left out, and the fifth is on hi-hat. I'm just using the clave rhythm and dispersing those accents around various voices. Sometimes I leave some out and sometimes it stays intact. This is how you customize a beat to make it your own—you have fun playing around with it until you get something that suits the song.

Example 43E: Rising Red Lung (ending tag 2:26)

When we play this song live, it keeps evolving and so I've altered what I did in the studio to help bolster that ending part to make it as exciting as possible (more like an event in the song). The basic character is still intact, but there are now a few little changes (the snare accent on the "+" of beat 2 is slid back and now happens on beat 3). This turns the clave into more of a 3:3 pattern, which is now closer to a calypso beat than a second line.

Example 43F: Live Adaptation

For comparison's sake, let's check out a basic calypso as well. I first learned this beat playing drums in a steel drum band in college. Calypso and its close cousin, the soca, come from the Caribbean and originally from the islands of Tobago and Trinidad. Like the second-line beat, these styles also have their roots in African drumming brought over to the Americas with the slave trade.

Example 43G: Basic Calypso

WEEK 44

WHOLE LOVE

Wilco from *The Whole Love*

For this song, I'm going to go a little beyond the established scope of this book and cover three sections, or three different beats, instead of just one (since they somewhat relate to the same idiom). That is jazz—specifically bop and big band drumming. Let's first start with the verse beat. This song is in a swung, triplet-based feel. I wanted to avoid riding on the cymbal or hi-hat so it wouldn't overtly sound like a shuffle. Instead, I chose to ride on the floor tom. The ride pattern is a mix of triplet rhythms. This is supplemented with a snare drum back beat on beats 2 and 4. Since the floor tom already covers some of the lower frequencies of the kit, I chose not to add the bass drum as an essential part of the beat. Instead, I saved it for the choruses where its sudden appearance would have more of an impact.

Let's check out the verse beat with a few variations as well.

Example 44A: Whole Love (0:16)

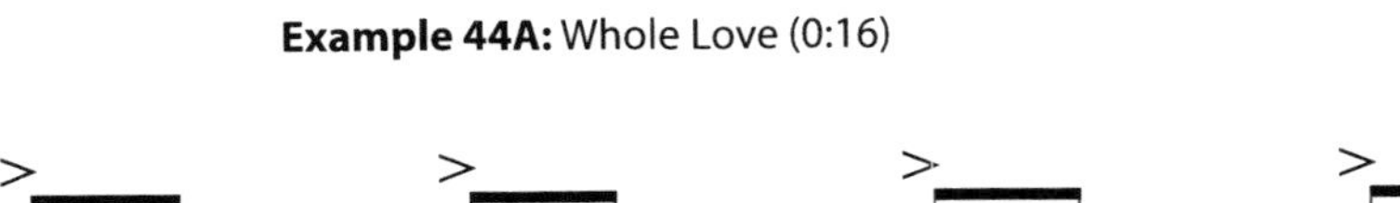

Example 44B: Ride Variation

The variation here is just mixing up what the right-hand ride part is doing on the floor tom, and adding or subtracting a snare note here or there on the last part of the triplet after any given back beat.

The chorus portion of the song is more of a traditional shuffle with accents thrown in on the ride (second floor tom) to support the vocal rhythm. To better illustrate this, here's a super stripped down shuffle with accents on the back beats.

Example 44C: Basic Shuffle

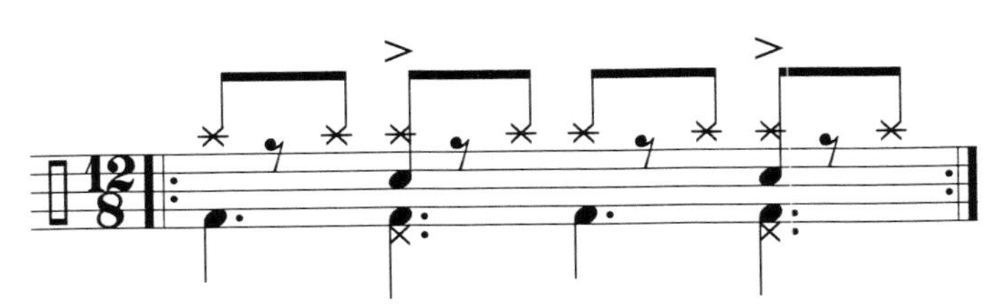

And, here's another popular basic shuffle. This variation has the snare drum doubling the ride part by playing the first and third subdivision of every triplet. The unaccented notes are played much lower (almost like ghost notes), as compared to the back beats. Using a whipping motion or Moeller stroke can help get the stick from the lower inner beat up to the accent a bit easier.

Example 44D: Shuffle Variation

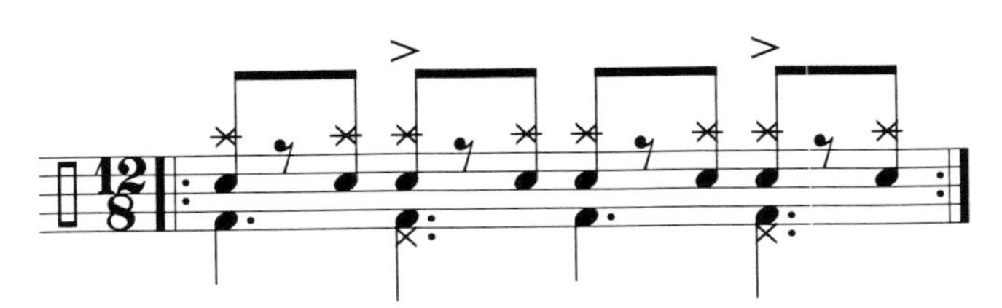

A Moeller stroke is a stroke that leads from the butt end of the stick, as opposed to the tip of the stick. So, where the tip of the stick is usually the first part to be lifted away from the head in preparation for the next stroke, with the Moeller stroke the end of the stick leads and the tip follows, creating that whipping motion. In my years of participating in marching percussion sections, I'm forever grateful that I was introduced to these techniques and concepts that include the Gladstone and Moeller strokes, the rudimental system, and the straight system. And, I'm also grateful I learned techniques from other areas of percussion as well, such as the Hinger timpani stroke, the Burton and Musser four-mallet vibraphone and marimba grips, the Spencer rotational marimba stroke, the German and French timpani grips, and the myriad of hand-drumming strokes and techniques. In my professional experience, all of these have proven valuable to know. Even if I'm rarely, if ever, required to implement these techniques, I have them at my disposal when I need to utilize them to play more effectively. The understanding of these disparate techniques allows me to better understand all of drumming in general and makes me better at what I do. I highly recommend learning as many techniques as possible even if it's something that seems impractical to what you're interested in (like a drumset player learning bodhran technique). You may never know just how positively it can impact your playing, but I guarantee it will in some way.

Now, let's check out the ride-cymbal variation. In this beat several of the accents moved from supporting the back beat to the third subdivision of the triplet (or the upbeats). This is directly influenced from studying jazz and bebop drumming. I was fortunate to have several gifted teachers who showed me how different a tune can feel by how the ride-cymbal pattern is interpreted. I still remember my very first lesson with Paul Wertico. I had loads of questions and concepts I wanted to touch upon and since this was the most expensive lesson I had ever taken (Paul was already an eight-time Grammy winner), I wanted to cram in as much as possible. The entire 60 plus minutes of that first lesson was spent entirely on the basic ride-cymbal pattern. I only used my right hand for the entire lesson! He wanted to make sure my ride pattern felt as good as possible by utilizing the right stroke, rebound, rhythmic interpretation and, most importantly, sound. He knew if I didn't have that together, the rest would never lock in and really swing.

Some of my other teachers around that time, such as Bob Rummage and Joel Spencer, introduced me to different ways of interpreting that basic ride pattern depending on what kind of tune I was playing. Sometimes the emphasis or accents fell on beats 2 and 4, sometimes it was more even with every downbeat receiving equal weight, and then there was the Elvin Jones interpretation. This put the emphasis on the upbeats of 2 and 4 giving the groove a forward momentum and motion that really resonated with drummers and musicians. That always stuck with me and so when I heard Jeff Tweedy's vocal rhythm and upbeat strumming pattern for the chorus of this song, it came naturally to me to emphasis those upbeats (á la Elvin).

Example 44E: Ride Accent Variation

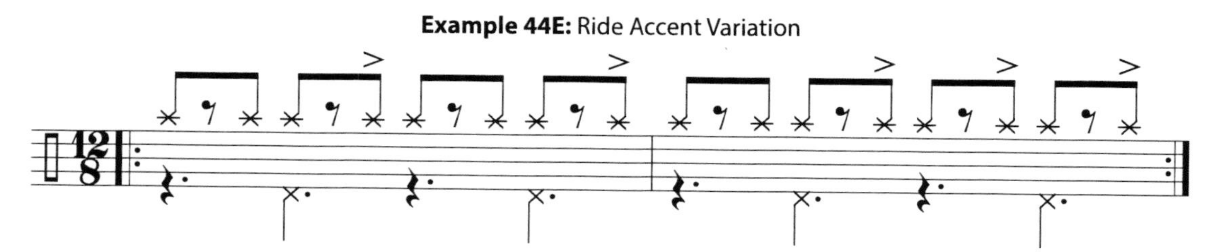

Now, let's add quarter notes in the feet and a snare drum back beat, and play the ride part on the floor tom. The addition of the back beat takes it firmly out of the world of bebop and more into the world of R&B (or the big band shout chorus). Both live and in the studio, I use a jingle ring on the hi-hat since it only sounds in the choruses. The addition of that new color gives a little more lift to my part. I also use an overturned drumhead resting on top of the floor tom head when I play this live so the floor-tom ride rhythms really get articulated and don't get lost in the low drone of the drum.

Example 44F: Chorus (0:30)
Full Beat

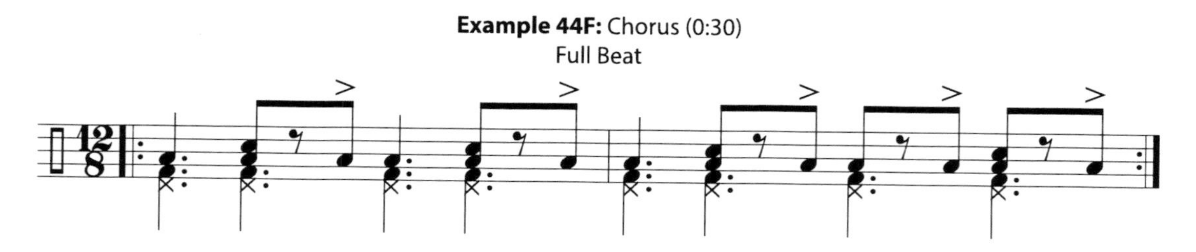

The next section we'll cover is from the bridge of "Whole Love." This is an active part emphasizing the accents the rest of the band plays. I first learned the concept I use here in big band drumming in order to set up figures in the music. More specifically, it's taken from a concept called the right-hand lead (or left-hand lead if you're a lefty). Steve Houghton turned me on to this concept and it completely put my big band drumming at a new level. It's basically supporting the band accents with the cymbal, which in turn is reinforced by the bass drum. The snare drum can then fill-in many or all of the other (supportive) notes or subdivisions that aren't accented. This not only rhythmically grounds what you're playing, but also helps to keep the rest of the band comfortable and tight by providing all of the sonic information necessary for the definitive placement of any group hits or accents. To begin with, here is an example with just the accents.

Example 44G: Bridge Hits

Now add the snare drum which plays on beat 3 (instead of beats 2 and 4), therefore implying a half-time feel. The half-time feel helps differentiate and give a unique characteristic to the bridge.

Example 44H: Hits with Snare Drum

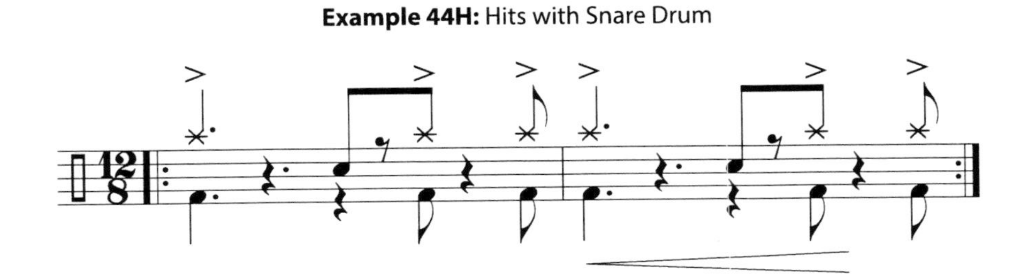

And, finally, the full-bridge beat as I play it.

Example 44I: Fill Bridge with Stickings and Hits (1:20)

R L R L R L R L R L L R R L R L R L R L R L L R

There is one more variation of this part, and that's what I play on the outro or coda of the song. It's similar to the bridge beat but is only one measure long and closer to the second half of that bridge beat.

Example 44J: Ending Variation (3:13)

CHAPTER 12

Beats with Brushes

WEEK 45

TRIGGER

birddog from *Ghost of the Season*

This is easily one of my favorite Birddog songs. It has a moody, dark, and almost nostalgic air about it brought out by Bill Santen's vocals and acoustic guitar, Steve Poulton's bass, Chris Tesluk's cello playing, and Megan Pickerel's backing vocals. The collage of tone color and use of space by those great musicians required something unique. Sticks would have been too distracting for that mood. I needed to use brushes with the snares off. Specifically, my favorite brushes, one of my most prized musical possessions. I found these brushes in an old store in Rib Lake, WI They are some kind of antique, seemingly homemade nylon brushes—shorter than most and with unfinished wooden handles. These are super-quiet brushes that sound pretty incredible when played like a stick (both striking the drum, and/or sliding on it). I use them extensively in the studio. They're on records with Jim O'Rourke, Wilco, Simon Joyner, Loose Fur, Loft Pillars, etc. The drumming is sparse in this song. The use of bass drum is minimal and there are only a few cymbal textures, such as a perpendicular hit on the edge of the crash cymbal to produce a bell-like ringing sound, some controlled impacts on the cymbal, and light hi-hat splashes acting as subtle, orchestral-inspired cymbal crashes. If you only have one cymbal, you quickly learn how many different sounds you can get from hitting it in certain spots with certain implements, the way in which it's struck, the number of fingers gripping the stick, or the part of the stick or implement that you're using. When isolated, you realize how all of these factors go into shaping a sound.

Since we often toured in rental cars or Bill's Camry (the van came later), I used a cocktail bass drum fashioned from a floor tom with an inverted bass drum pedal, and a thick double-ply Evans hydraulic head on the bottom batter side (the inverted pedal idea came straight from Maureen Tucker). The bass and snare were the only drums. I often used the top floor tom head as a second snare drum, splitting back beat parts up between the two drums. In place of having several different drum and cymbal options, I instead relied on a lot of different types of implements to get different sounds and effects out the drums, hi-hat, and cymbal I used. Implements and small percussion instruments were my adaptations in that setting and, as usual, limitations proved to be fruitful.

It was incredible how differently it would sound and feel to play a song with either taped up blasticks, rods, nylon brushes, rods that I made out of broom bristles (before Pro-Mark starting manufacturing those), taped up wire brushes with coins affixed to them, or wooden dowels with felt or moleskin wrapped around the ends. All of these elicited strikingly different timbres, and each made me play a little bit differently since I was obviously reacting to the nuances of the implements that are ostensibly extensions of our arms and hands in the first place.

Small percussion items became alternatives to different cymbals or drums. I used sheep bells as shakers to get more of a raw "ride-cymbal" sound. Or, sometimes just shook a small hand bell to create a drone in a chorus since the whole idea of the jazz ride in the first place was to create a washy, sonic bed for the other instruments to improvise over. The riding we do in rock music is just an outgrowth of that, so why not try other kinds of drones? I also used small measuring cups and brass ashtrays that could be mounted near the edge of my snare drum using Velcro. I would sometimes use these as a surface to ride on, or just fill in the rests between back beats with these metallic, indefinitely pitched sounds.

All of these examples are being shared in hopes that you can filter these experiences through your own, and potentially use some of these ideas and concepts as triggers (or jumping off points) for personal musical and artistic expression.

For "Trigger," my right hand strikes the snare (snares off!) with the brushes on beat 1, and then does small counter-clockwise circles on counts 2 and 3. My left hand sweeps small clockwise circles on all three beats. The bass drum then adds a sparse pulse. In the mixing of this song, my snare drum was run through a Sans Amp effect, making the brushes even grittier and slightly distorted. That was something I was for since all too often brushes imply quiet, respectful background playing. There's a lot more to brushes than that. It's a shame how brush playing has almost become a lost art. I feel they haven't even been fully explored yet, as there's still a lot to discover with these tools.

For this beat, I suggest you first play it with your hands acting as the brushes. Slide them and see what kind of sounds you get by adjusting the pressure, or by how much of your hands are in contact with the head at certain points in the motion cycle. The bass drum part (notated here) is merely representative of the part, which isn't set—it's always moving around and thinning out depending on the rhythm of the vocal line and the dynamics.

Example 45A: Trigger

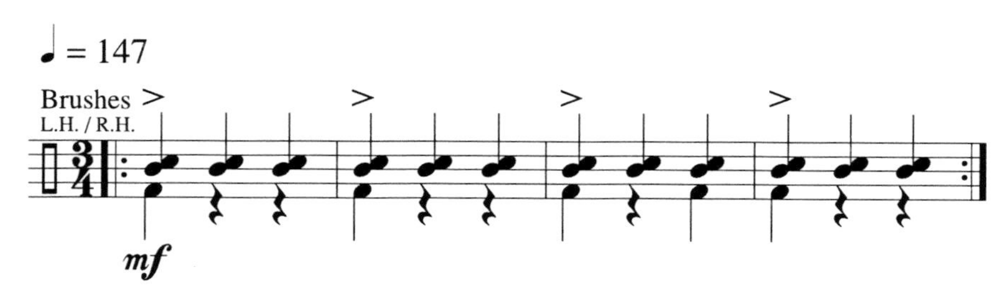

Note that the "snare hit" is on count 1 instead of beats 2 or 3, which is typical in $\frac{3}{4}$ time. I did this because the subject matter of the song is heavy. I didn't want it to be a waltz or light. By putting the back beat on 1, it robbed the groove of its affability.

LIFE GOES OFF

Jim O'Rourke from *Insignificance*

Where do I start with this one? A few considerations right off the bat might help. Jim is fond of trying to stump me. Not out of maliciousness or for the sake of stumping, he just always has a lot of ideas and a clear vision of how a song should go. Sometimes he's hearing these multiple ideas in quick succession and ends up asking me something like, "Okay, can you play this rhythm with your snare drum and the other with your bass drum? And, when we change from playing in three to playing in four, can you keep it in three and then somehow make the phrase line up at the next section?" That's actually an example of an easier request of his. I always oblige and say yes, even if I can't do it! I know if I write it out and get a second to work on it, I can most likely pull it off (or something close).

This brings me to a point I'd like to make. I've found the ability to read music beyond valuable in my musical experience. Even though I'm rarely required to read the music I've been making the last 20 years, it's been an incredible tool for me to utilize. When you're able to read, you can often just hear something and immediately visualize how it would look written down. That gives me a mental picture to come back to so I don't forget what it is I'm either supposed to play, or that I wanted to play. Even if I never write it down, I not only have an aural memory of it, but a visual memory as well. Of course there are plenty of incredible musicians who never learned to read music nor needed to learn. Buddy Rich is the most famous example amongst drummers. But many rock musicians don't read either. It doesn't hold many of them back and, in fact, an argument can be made that it frees them up from the constraints of formal music making. But in my position, as a drummer trying to elevate each song I play (which sometimes means managing complicated requests from the artists I work with), reading music has only been an asset, and never a hindrance. When I was playing in several different bands before joining Wilco, I had to keep track of hundreds of songs in my head. Having little sketched music notation charts and notes allowed me to get right into the song and not have to worry about the beat. Instead, it allowed me to concentrate on my other responsibilities, including time, tempo, sound, playing to the room, and being supportive to the other musicians. I've written this book with enough balance between notation and words so drummers and musicians who don't read drumset notation can still hopefully garner some lessons or insights from my shared experience. But, if you do read music, you can get the full experience of what I'm talking about in these pages.

Getting back to "Life Goes Off," this is an example of Jim searching for a sound and using me to help get it. He wanted a super tight bass drum sound since the acoustic guitar and voice are the focal points of the song. Instead of using a bass drum at all, Jim pulled out the little green vinyl suitcase he used for touring and to carry gear in. We stood it up on its side and put the bass drum pedal right up to it, miked it, and it was perfect. I then played those favorite antique nylon brushes of mine on the top of the suitcase, which acted as a snare drum. That was my kit. That's all it needed. There's an impossibly fast brush sixteenth note snare drum drone that happens as an effect in parts of the song too. But that was overdubbed and not part of the actual beat for the song.

First, let's just examine what the hands are doing. It's a simple waltz feel with the back beat falling on the second note of each three-note grouping.

Example 46A: Life Goes Off
Hands

♩. = 66
Brushes
R.H. / L.H.

Now, let's just see how the right foot and left hand are interacting.

Example 46B: Bass Drum and Left-Hand Brush

And now, let's put it all together. This is the beat heard in the second half of the verses (as well as the chorus), even though the guitar switches to playing in four. This creates a 4 against 3 feel that is resolved at the end of the phrase by just adding an extra beat to the end of the last drum measure.

Example 46C: Full Beat (0:17)

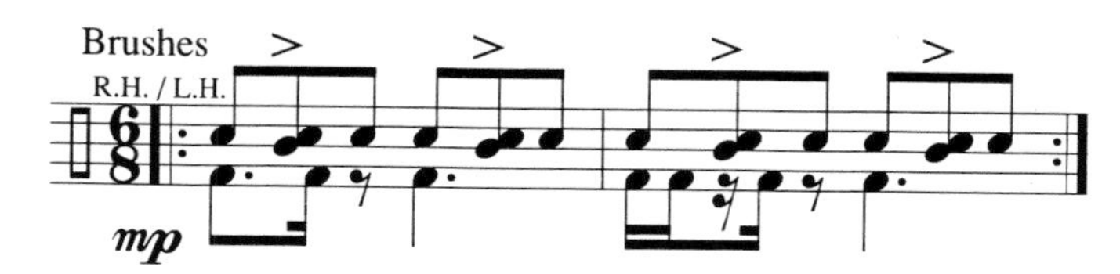

WEEK 47

A CHANGE OF HEART

7 Worlds Collide from *The Sun Came Out*

New Zealand based singer-songwriter Bic Runga was one of the incredible musicians I had the pleasure of working with on Neil Finn's 7 Worlds Collide charity project. This is a song she wrote and asked John Stirratt and I to be the rhythm section for. It's a classic, heartbreaking, slow country-style waltz. I'm so happy that my wife, Miiri, turned me on to the music of Patsy Cline. She had some incredible songs with this type of feel and I felt that listening to those so many times helped me understand the sensitivity and feel that Bic was going for on this beautiful song.

As in "Trigger" (week 45), I play clockwise circles with the left-hand brush and counterclockwise circles with my right brush. Keep the snares off on this one as well. I heard brush master Ed Thigpen once say to keep the snares off when playing brushes. I'm not one for absolutes, but I do find that brushes with the snares off can blend better in a gentle song with acoustic guitar and intimate vocals. I used a vintage marching bass drum on this recording, and its sound is very deep and open. I reserve it for the downbeat of each measure. The left-hand circle dominates the drumhead for beat 1, while the right-hand circles are larger and more dominant on counts 2 and 3. So, think of it as left, right, right and you'll begin to picture what it looks like.

Example 47A: Change of Heart (Verse)

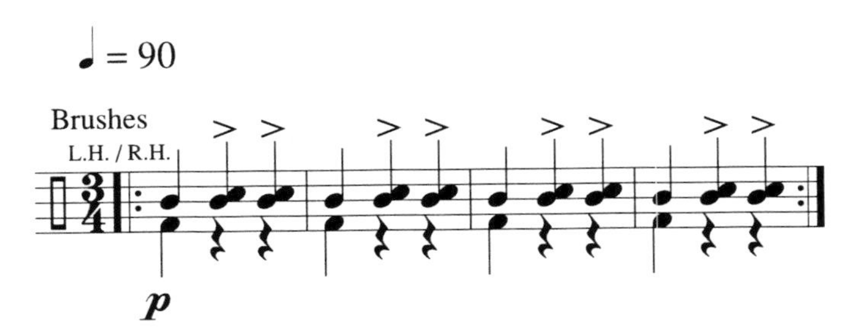

For the bridge of this song, I play a slight variation. I add more of a tap (or stroke) with the right hand on beat 3 instead of a sliding circle pattern. This gives a bit more lift and weight to an otherwise purely supportive beat. For this variation, you can think left, right, tap. Two drums and brushes are all you need for this beat.

Example 47B: Bridge Part (1:46)

MUZZLE OF BEES

Wilco from *A Ghost Is Born*

This song is always fun to play for several reasons, one being the challenge that comes with using three different implements during the course of the song. For this verse part, I use a brush with a coin affixed to it in my right hand, and a hotrod bundle stick in my left that has a ping pong ball partially filled with shotgun shot affixed to the butt end. The shaker attached to the rod gives a little more brightness to each stroke so it can cut through better. This beat has two distinct halves.

The first half is a straight 2 and 4 beat. The right brush keeps time with light eighth-note taps on the snare head, while the left-hand rod supplies the back beat. The bass drum plays on 1 and 3, and the hi-hat on 2 and 4. For the second half, the snare follows the fingerpicking guitar accents while the feet remain the same. Let's first take a look at the entire beat. The accents in parentheses are half accents, notes with a little more weight but not necessarily popping out over the rest of the beat.

Example 48A: Muzzle of Bees (0:19)

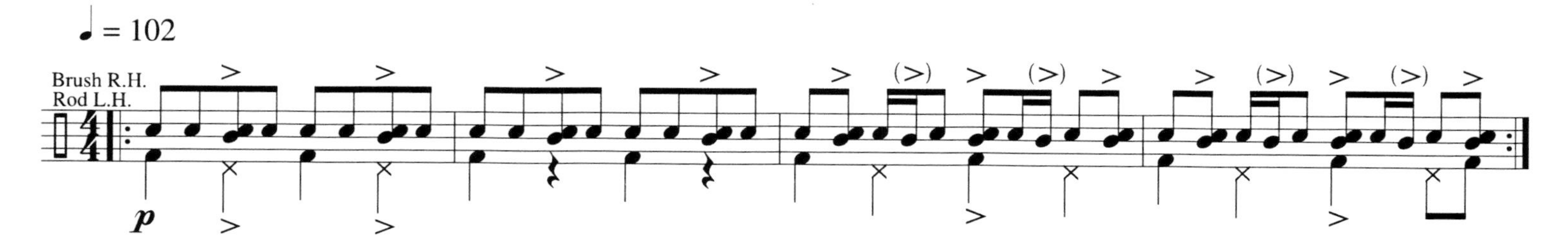

One thing to keep in mind that the written beat doesn't quite convey is that I ever so slightly swing the third and fourth bars. I just give those little syncopated figures a little lilt, but nothing overtly swung. Just a little buoyancy as Nels Cline would say. Another thing to keep in mind is that at those spots where the right and left hands are written as playing in unison in the third and fourth bars, I'm actually flamming them a bit. These are left-hand flams with the brush providing the grace note, and the rod playing the primary note. I usually play them on the wide side with the grace note higher than I would normally have it, so it provides a fatter sound.

The third and fourth measures feature a syncopated 3 against 4 figure. The feet are keeping the beat firmly planted in $\frac{4}{4}$ time, but the hands are playing every third note. This is what the hands alone look like.

Example 48B: Hands Only

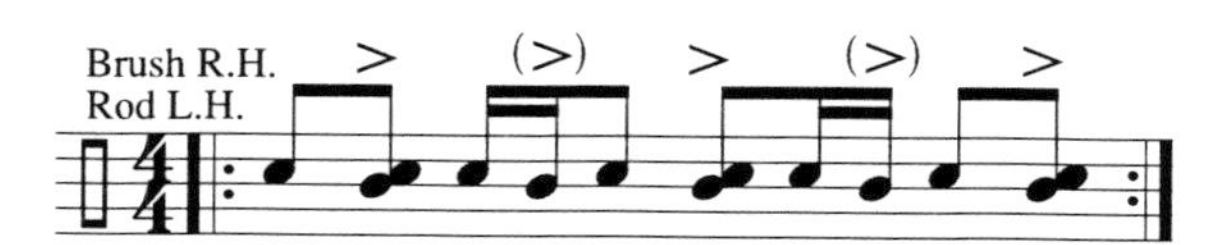

And, here it is written all on one line (as if it were snare drum music).

Example 48C: Hands Only on One Surface

Sometimes it's fun to play around with the 3 against 4 figure. This is the same rhythm, but instead of the repeating three-subdivision grouping beginning with two rests and then one note, this three-note grouping example begins with the note and is followed by two rests. It's the same thing, just shifted.

Example 48D: Hemiola Shifted

And, of course, you could start the three-note grouping with one rest, then one note, and then the third rest as well. I've found it practical and fun to practice cross rhythms like this (that's what I like to call them), starting on each possible subdivision. This helps in that when you hear something in your head and want to play it in the moment, your muscles have already worked it out. So, the coordination between limbs is already inherent. This will hopefully keep you from getting tripped up when you throw an idea out spontaneously in order to interact with what someone else is playing.

CHAPTER 13

Beats Associated with Programmed Beats

WEEK 49

STARVE THEM TO DEATH

Sean Watkins from *Blinders On*

This was originally a programmed beat Sean came up with himself. Since the songwriter often has an idea of what type of groove he or she hears for a particular song, I like to start with any suggestions or demos they have and work from there. For this song, Sean nailed it. The programmed beat was really interesting, so I decided to just learn it, and then added some more human variations.

The programmed beat has some elements you don't hear every day, like the cross rhythm between the hi-hat ride and the bass drum upbeat pattern. This isn't something I would have necessarily come up with on my own, or the first place a drummer would have gone. So, when I came up with variations, I not only grew as a drummer by opening some new doors for my playing, but also as a musician by trying to present the given material in as human and musical way as possible. This first example is the actual programmed beat:

Example 49A: Starve Them to Death
Programmed Beat

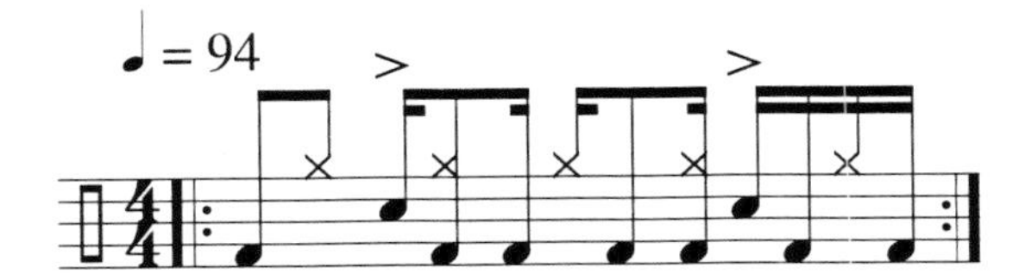

This second example is a variation. I threw in some ghost notes, which end up making it feel a bit better and more performed than programmed. But it also makes it easier to play since more rhythmic information actually helps to anchor the three-note grouped hi-hat part (a three-note hemiola). Therefore, filling in the two consecutive rests with ghost notes allows the eighth notes to flow more easily, and helps to keep the upbeat bass drum pattern more stable.

Example 49B: Human Variation (0:05)

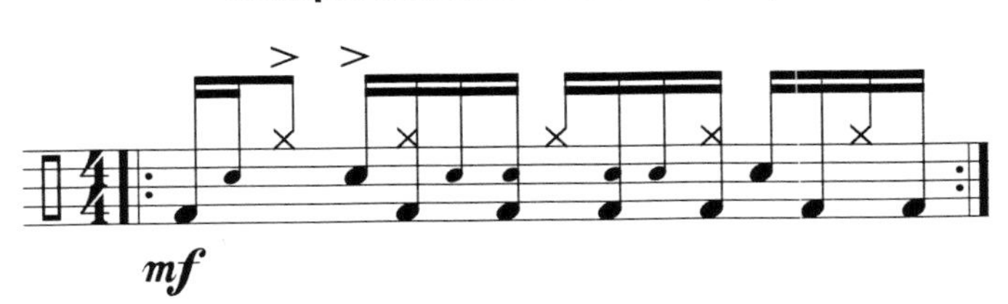

The last variation is something I came up with just in case the other beat wasn't working. This one features hand-to-hand sixteenth notes on the hi-hat, keeping the original hi-hat part as accents but now with the other subdivisions filled in. This also has a grounding effect on the whole beat.

Example 49C: Bridge Variation (1:46)

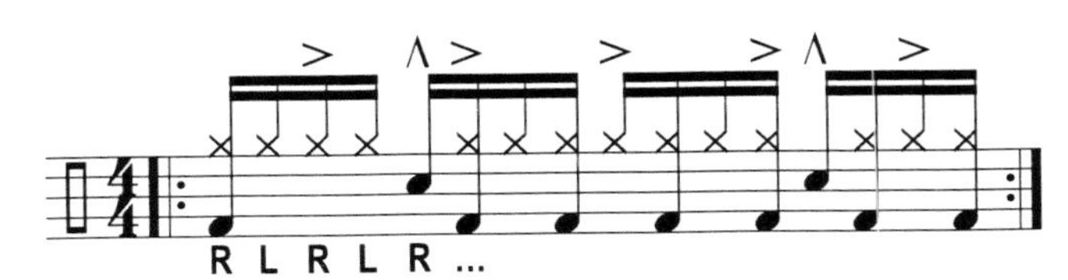

I ended up using all three grooves on the track. I start with the live kit version of the programmed beat, moved to variation #1 for the second verse, and use variation #2 for the solo. These slight changes in the groove may not be very noticeable sonically, but they do have a significant effect on feel and how well all of the parts stick together.

WEEK 50

HEAVY METAL DRUMMER

Wilco from *Yankee Hotel Foxtrot*

This is a song that had a demo drum part created on an MPC (Music Production Controller) that worked really well, so I just added some supplemental drums. The MPC part comes and goes throughout, hence the need for something consistent that plays through the entire song. My part is a fairly straight ahead four-bar pattern, with the exception of a little turnaround at the end of each phrase that mimics the MPC part.

Example 50A: Heavy Metal Drummer (0:02)

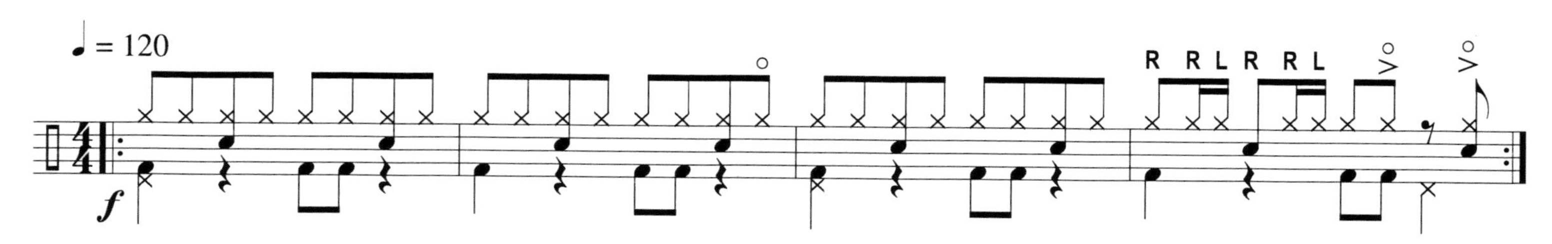

WEEK 51

MAKEOUT

Matt Marque from *Nothing Personal*

Here's an example of a song that was basically finished, and I was brought in to add live drums along to an existing drum machine part. As is similar to the two previous beats, I came up with something closely related to the programmed part but a bit more organic. I enter on the chorus of the song, playing the ride cymbal and overdubbing the shaker to contrast and open up the tight, programmed verse.

Example 51A: Makeout (0:52)

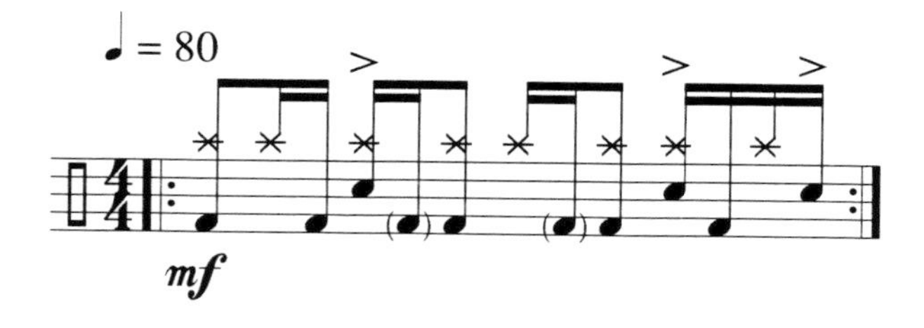

I also add a post-chorus beat that starts with a thirty-second note figure on the hi-hat, as well as a hi-hat opening emphasizing the upbeat of count 2. It's a variation that keeps the snare drum and bass drum part intact.

Example 51B: Variation (1:16)

WEEK 52

PROJECTIONS OF (WHAT) MIGHT . . .

Glenn Kotche from *Mobile*

Two master percussionists inspired this piece—Afro beat founding father Tony Allen, and jazz legend Edward Blackwell. After copious amounts of time spent listening to these fabulous players, I was playing around with some of their beats while practicing one day and began to personalize and change them up a bit. After doing so, I came up with several of my own variations, using their original beats as blueprints. I did things like adding tuned cowbell parts or different cross-rhythm foot patterns, and messing around with different voicings and stickings. I then notated and collaged these various beats and enhanced them electronically to create this piece for my third solo record, *Mobile*. What we'll focus on here is one of my favorite beats from the piece, and another that's a close relative of it.

Since these beats seem to be tough for most people at first, let's start incrementally and build up all of the necessary coordination that's required of the full beat. We begin with just a buildup of what the ostinato left hand and right foot will provide. I've written it here with a kind of check pattern as the first measure.

A check pattern is something I learned to do first in the Lake Park High School marching band drum line, with my fantastic high school drum teacher, Mike Chiodo and, later, with Bret Kuhn in The Cavaliers Drum and Bugle Corps snare line. (I must interject that I was really lucky for having access to so many incredible drum teachers growing up. I can't imagine where I'd be without them.) A check pattern is the same idea as the control in a scientific experiment. It's the skeleton of a pattern that is played preceding that pattern as a way to establish the timing, feel, and interpretation correctly. This way you can directly compare a pattern over and over against something that is simpler and steady. In this example, the check pattern is just a measure of alternating eighth notes between the snare drum and bass drum. This sets up the timing for the alternating sixteenth-note doubles in the following measure.

Example 52A: Projections of (What) Might
Check Pattern

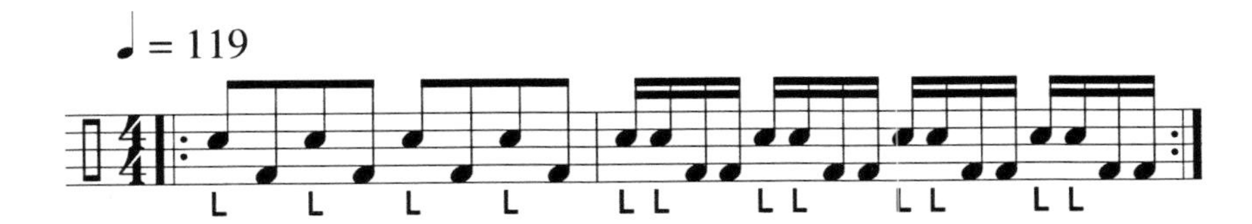

So, once you have those doubles between the snare and bass drum feeling good, it's time to orchestrate the left hand between three surfaces. I play this beat beginning with the snare drum, moving to the rack tom and floor toms, respectively, and then cycling it over again. You can start the left-hand pattern on any drum as long as the basic idea of using three surfaces remains intact (this grouping of three pitches will work well against the cowbell pattern in four later on). Let's just try this in $\frac{3}{4}$ time at first, keeping in mind that the left-hand doubles will feel slightly different on each of the three drums since their head tension and diameters will be different. I suggest trying to stroke the doubles as much as possible instead of trying to bounce them. Stroking them means using more finger control and relying less on the rebound of the head. Think of it as two little finger strokes instead of one wrist stroke with stick rebound. The result is usually a more even sounding and rhythmically defined double stroke.

Example 52B: Snare Drum and Bass Drum Doubles

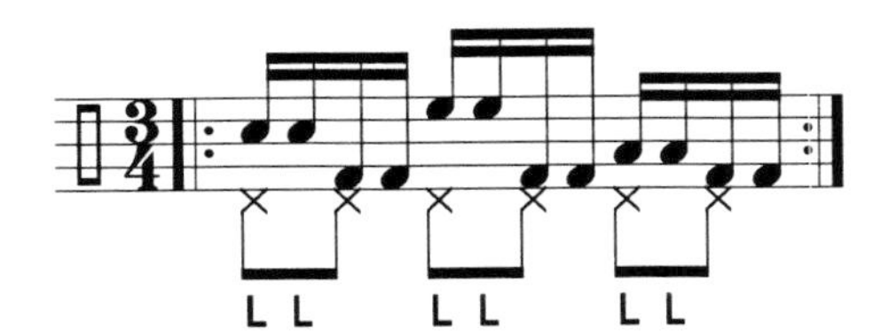

This pattern will take four cycles or repetitions to match up with the cowbell pattern. So, let's try it. Four repetitions will work out to be two measures of $\frac{6}{4}$, which is the time signature and length of the final beat.

Example 52C: Left-Hand Part with Bass Drum and Hi-Hat

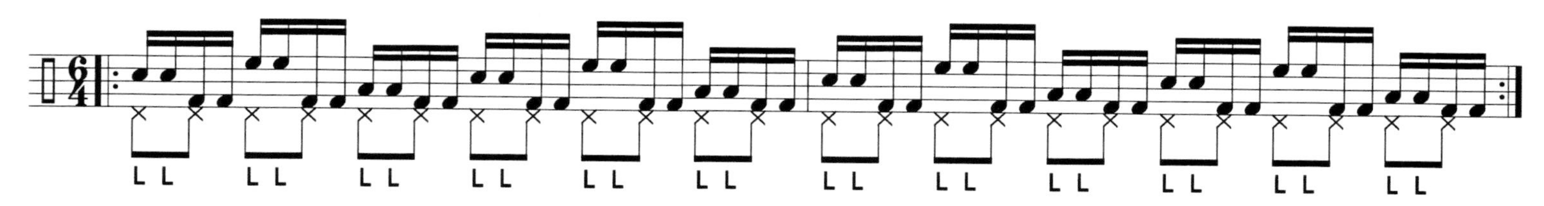

Next, let's switch to the cowbell pattern. This is a four-beat pattern split up among three different pitched cowbells. Feel free to use other instruments as well—as long as there are three distinct pitch areas, the beat will translate (I use three almglocken on the recording and live – g# 2 / g# 3 / a# 3). Begin with just getting the rhythm down on one surface.

Example 52D: Bell Part Rhythm

Now you can try it on three bells. The letters over the notes provide a little help denoting high, medium, and low pitches.

Example 52E: Bell Melody

Let's try the same thing with the addition of the hi-hat eighth notes in the left foot (the anchor!).

Example 52F: With Hi-Hat "Anchor"

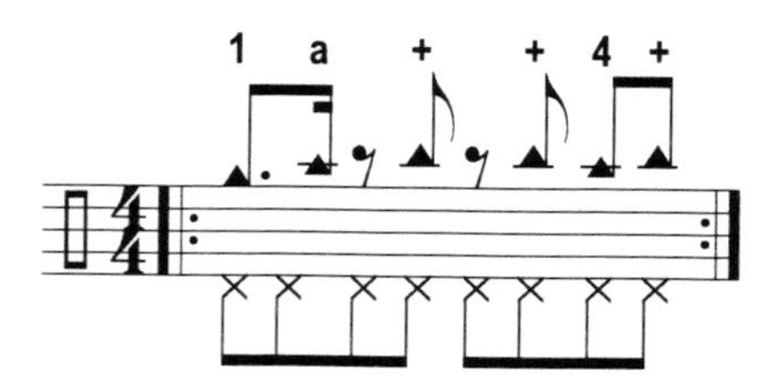

Since the bell pattern is four beats long, it will cycle three times in a two-measure phrase of $\frac{6}{4}$ time. Thinking this way is just basic math. Two measures of $\frac{6}{4}$ have a total of 12 beats. Three cycles of four equals 12 beats. And, for the left hand and bass drum pattern, four cycles of three also equals 12.

Example 52G: Full Melodic Cycle

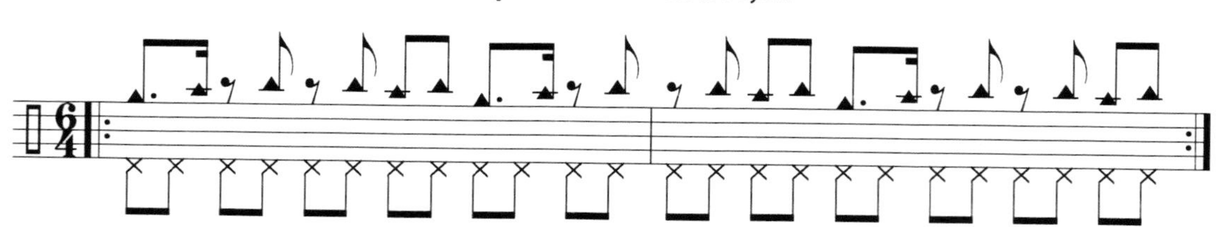

Now comes the fun! Try that same bell pattern against the other three limbs. You have the hi-hat grounding everything with solid eighth notes in the left foot. For now, the left hand will remain on the snare drum and alternating eighth notes with the bass drum.

Example 52H: Snare Drum and Bass Drum Doubles

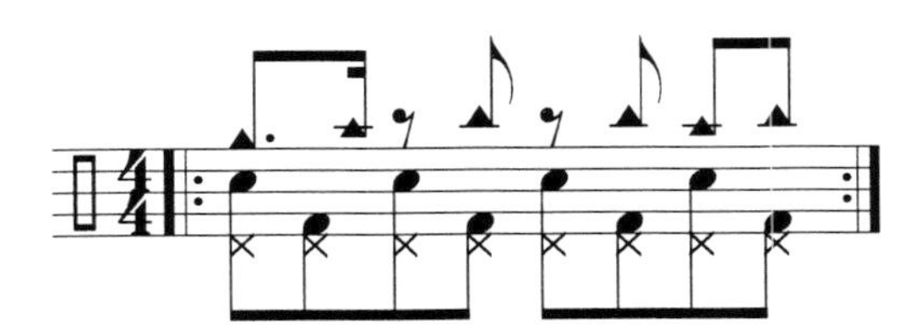

Now try the same thing with the addition of sixteenth-note doubles between the snare and bass drum.

Example 52I: Melody with Simplified Left-Hand Voicings

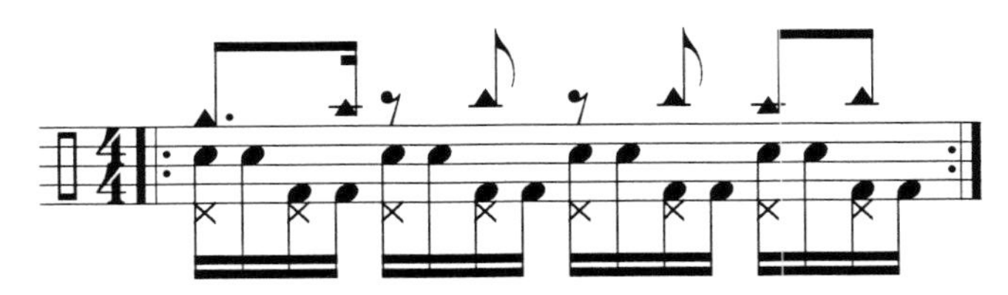

Next you have the snare and toms alternating eighth notes with the bass drum. Therefore, all of the left hand and right foot notes will match up with the hi-hat. This is the first time you'll hear the polyrhythmic melody of the bell pattern in four, and the left-hand snare drum and toms in three, all sounding concurrently. Keep in mind that those two parts will only match up every two measures in $\frac{6}{4}$.

Example 52J

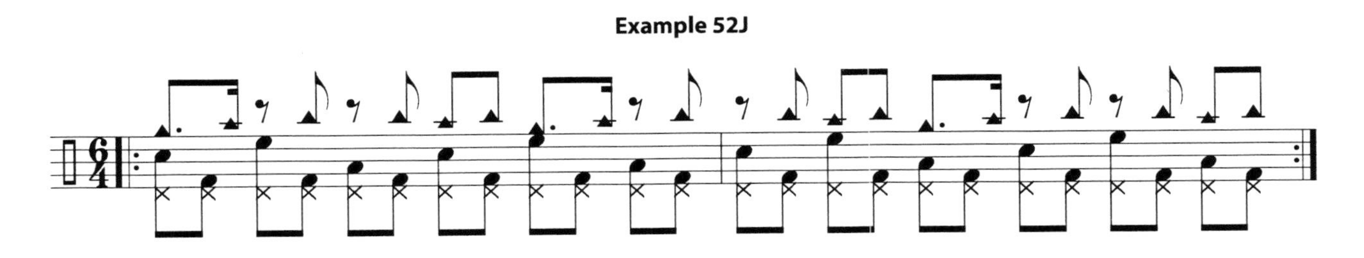

Finally, you're ready to put it all together. Every two measures you'll hear it all line up again. Start slow and if you're having trouble, build the right-hand bell part up one pitch at a time while you keep the other three limbs cycling.

Example 52K: Full Beat (0:48)

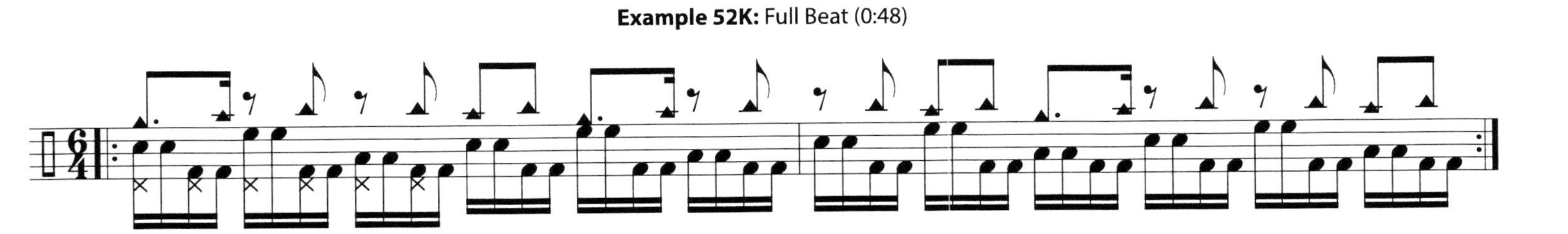

I encourage you to experiment with your own variations of this beat. One of my favorite variations is almost the same but with one small change. The rhythm and melody of the bell pattern is different. This variation still uses three pitched bells, but the third bell note comes one sixteenth note earlier. There's one more eighth-note bell added on count 3. The other three limbs are exactly the same as in Ex. 52K.

Example 52L: Variation

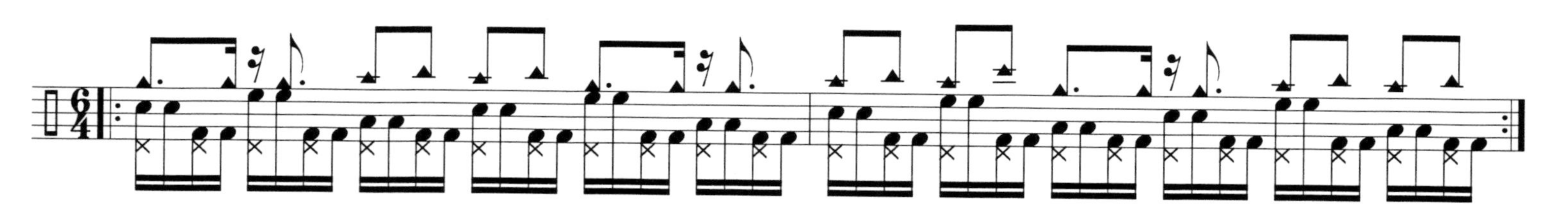

Enjoy working these out and remember, even though you may never play these beats in a professional situation, by learning the fundamentals and mechanics inherent in each beat, you're acquiring the mental and physical skills that will help you create your own original rhythmic expressions and musical statements. Thank you for checking all of these beats out!